Endorsements

As a life coach, personal trainer, fitness instructor, travel agent, and professional organizer, this is a must read! I recommend *A Year of Mindful Wellness* to all my clients and colleagues. This book was so inspiring, it felt like it was written just for me! It will be my go-to guide for living mindfully for many years to come.

— Debbie Rosenberg, owner of Deb on Holiday, certified fitness instructor and personal trainer

Lisa puts her heart into this very well written guide to mindfulness. The step by step format is a great hands-on approach to have mindfulness in your life on a daily basis. I love the way she adds simplicity to some very complex ideas. This is a must-have for your bedside table.

— Sylvia Crossland, Yoga teacher and Realtor

Lisa Feder's book provides a remedy for people like me who recognize the need for a change but may not know where to begin.

Each chapter provides practical strategies for learning and applying mindfulness to our daily lives, whether it be at home, at work, or with our family and friends. Her approachable writing style is from her heart and is based on her personal experience, knowledge, and research on this subject.

Thank you, Lisa, for writing this book and helping us to learn how to live in and appreciate the present and lead a healthy, mindful life.

— Leslie Katz, marketing director

Lisa shares an easy-to-digest, "mindfulness-for-dummies" presentation that takes the mystery out of living in the moment! A truly helpful, perspective-changing read that will impact the way you look at your world.

— Allison Schwartz, interior designer

In *A Year of Mindful Wellness,* Lisa offers simple, manageable ways to incorporate wellness into everyday life. This book is designed for people who are already familiar with, or just dipping their toes into, the mindfulness stream, Lisa's sense of humor and her compassion shine through the pages of her book. If you are a human with stress, you will learn some new ways of thinking about and managing the stress in your life. And if you ever get a chance to take a class or join a retreat with Lisa, do it!

— Theresa Misenti, graphic designer

A Year of Mindful Wellness

Twelve months to stress less and live more

LISA FEDER

Being Well Yoga
Publishing

A Year of Mindful Wellness: Twelve months to stress less and live more.
Copyright © 2018 by Lisa Feder.

Editing and typesetting: Sally Hanan at Inksnatcher.com
Cover design: Les at fiverr.com/germancreative
Head shot photo: Debra Ellsworth at debrawellsworthphotography.com
Illustrations: Freyja Zazu at freyjazazuart.wordpress.com
Video: Charlotte Moore at Mooremediaco.com

Ordering Information:
Quantity sales. Special discounts are available on quantity purchases by corporations, associations, and others. For details, contact the author through the e-mail above.

A Year of Mindful Wellness: Twelve months to stress less and live more/Lisa Feder—first ed.
ISBN 978-1-7327657-0-2

This book is dedicated to Seth, Frank, and Zoë: my perfect reasons for wanting to be mindful.

Contents

I. Mindful Wellness 1

   1. Mindful Intentions 13

   2. Mindful Breath 21

   3. Mindful Movement 35

   4. Mindful Energy Management 57

   5. Mindful Media Detox 69

   6. Mindful Mornings and Evenings 81

   7. Mindful Nutrition 93

   8. Mindful Meditation Practices 109

   9. Mindful Communication 121

  10. Mindful Conflict Resolution 135

  11. Mindful Gratitude 145

  12. Mindful Self-Care for the Holidays ... 155

II. Mindfully Moving Forward 165

Acknowledgments 169

About the Author 172

Some Favorite Recipes 174

Preface

Here is my wish for you:

> *to be able to experience, create, and feel more;*
> *to be free to do less but accomplish more,*
> *to breathe more and stress less,*
> *to feel better and be healthier,*
> *to help yourself and to know that you are enough.*

And when you do, you will feel at home all the time, regardless of what you are dealing with. You will understand that being busy is not the same as moving intentionally through your life to accomplish what makes you happy. You will live in each moment of your life rather than feel that life has passed you by.

It doesn't happen immediately, which is why I am offering you *A Year of Mindful Wellness.* In the following chapters you will be invited to learn, inquire, and process various aspects of *mindful wellness.* These will serve you at home, at work, when you are by yourself, and when you are with others. You will have a supply of tools to keep you mindful and well, regardless of the challenges life throws your way.

Here's how to use this book:

- Why are you reading this? Write down what you would like to get out of this journey.
- Read the first chapter—it's an explanation of what mindful wellness is. There is also a review of what stress is, and an opportunity to look at the triggers that keep you feeling stressed rather than mindful.
- Then read the next twelve chapters—one for each month of the year—hence, *A Year of Mindful Wellness.* Feel free to either work through each chapter in order, or move through selectively or at a faster rate. Whatever you do, be sure to take time to practice your new habits so that they stick.
- Each chapter also has some self-inquiry exercises and some thought starters for you to design your path home to mindful wellness.

I hope that this book will help you find a new perspective and some healthy, mindful habits so you can stress less, breathe more, be present, and feel better.

Be well,
Lisa

Mindful Wellness

A new way to take care of your whole self

> *What lies behind us and what lies before us are tiny*
> *matters compared to what lies within us.*
> *– Henry S. Haskins*

A FEW YEARS AGO, I was a little lost. I have always been busy by nature and necessity, but I'd come to a time in my life when everything wasn't so urgent anymore. I'd spent the previous twenty years working full or part time while raising two kids; and in those days, my evenings were full too, or I was so exhausted I couldn't even move. But now things were different. With the kids away at college, I found myself with some open space. Yet in the evenings, when time finally stretched out ahead of me, I wasn't mindfully *home.* I needed to restore my sense of wholeness, but I wasn't sure how.

Most of my time during the day was spent thinking about, writing about, and teaching mindful practices. I taught (and still teach) Yoga and meditation, and I presented (and still present) workshops on bringing mindful practices to the workplace and everyday life. These practices had transformed my days, yet still, at the end of the day, I regressed to habits of distraction. I think I was driven by FOMO (fear of missing out), a mild addiction to busyness, and a feeling that I just hadn't quite done enough.

Distractions and more busyness were my solution, and life was good because I loved my work. But I felt this vague dissatisfaction that it wasn't enough. That I wasn't enough. I added more classes and took more trainings. I filled time with meetings and constant connection.

But there was still a missing piece. I was missing *mindful wellness.* I wasn't paying attention to every moment, rather, I was just filling it up. I found that when I paid attention—really, really paid attention, and restrained myself from just filling my time with my usual distractions—possibilities opened up. I discovered there was time to journal and meditate

2

and cook and think, and I began to remember things I would often forget in the throes of having too much to do. When I really practiced *mindful wellness*, I felt a sense of expansion—time for more, a feeling of being less rushed—and when I did less, I actually was able to experience, create, and feel more. And that led to being more productive. I did less and became more productive. It didn't seem possible, but it happened.

Don't miss the messages

Mindfulness is a state of paying attention to what is, as it is, and as it is happening. It is often referred to as "being present," which seems straightforward, but we know it is not. When we don't pay attention, we can miss things. We might arrive at our destination not really knowing how we got there. We might overlook a friend's call for help or lose our keys. We might miss and neglect important messages from others, resulting in lost or damaged relationships, challenges communicating, and unresolved conflict. If we neglect messages from our *selves*—from the body, the mind, or the spirit—it can result in injury, illness, depression, anxiety, and a whole host of other issues that keep us from feeling healthy and whole.

We miss things big and small, and over time, we can end up missing a large chunk of our lives.

I can't tell you how many times I've heard parents wish they had paid more attention to the little details of life when their kids were young ("Cat's in the Cradle," anyone?), or they were too busy "doing" to notice what was really happening.

Mindfulness is paying attention to all the "stuff" going on in the moment, and it's also paying attention to the moments in-between the stuff that is happening. So much of our lives is in these in-between moments. Waiting for a show to begin. Sitting in the doctor's office. In line to check out at the grocery. In the car, transitioning to the next activity. We don't pay attention, or we wish these in-between moments away. Claude DeBussey said, "Music is the space between the notes," but we don't notice the music. Instead, we fill the space with our conditioned thinking, emotions, past experiences, expectations, and ego, drowning out the "music" of our lives.

It's enough. You're enough

I was letting myself be constantly distracted by everything in the evenings: the need to check my e-mail, check for text messages, scroll through my Facebook feed. I'm not sure exactly what I was looking for, but it made me a little restless. I couldn't quite let go of the day. Then I'd jump up because I remembered something else I needed to do. I'd watch a little more TV, flip through a magazine, and check my phone again.

Now, on days when I allow or challenge myself to pay attention to myself, rather than distract myself from the moment I awaken, I notice a shift. I feel openness, yes, but also a connection to myself. I have an understanding that the day, and I, will be enough. I move through the day more clearly, allowing the dog to have a few more moments on the walk to sniff whatever she is sniffing before heading home. I tend to remember what I walked into a room for; rather than walking in, wondering why, and walking out, only to repeat the same fruitless activity later. I am more present in conversations and appreciate others more rather than become annoyed at small things. And yes, food tastes better, the sky is bluer, and the flowers are more vibrant—yes. I feel appreciation and gratitude for the ups and downs rather than getting caught up in their details. And I realize that e-mail holds no special answer for me, Facebook posts will not reveal the meaning of life, and watching the news will not necessarily enlighten me at all. I was spending too much time with those things, looking for something. Becoming mindful reveals to me that nothing is missing, so there is nothing to look for.

Wellness is the feeling of being okay. It is that feeling of wholeness and being at ease and at home with yourself. It is being satisfied that you are complete as you are, not needy or lacking in anything to be worthy of a full, satisfying life. So *mindful wellness* is about paying attention to what *is* so you can be present, address what needs attention, and feel complete. Sounds pretty good to me.

> *When you realize that nothing is lacking, the whole world belongs to you. — Lao Tzu*

A mindful approach to stress management

Stress is our fight or flight response to a demand or threat on the body or mind. This is fine for short-term battles we face; but with chronic or long-term stress, this leads to wear and tear on the body. In the US, 77 percent of people report regularly experiencing physical symptoms caused by stress, and 73 percent report regularly experiencing psychological symptoms.[1]

Stress can come from:

— the environment—noise, pollution, etc.;
— the body—when we are physically ill; or
— the mind.

Most of our stress is manufactured in our minds.

We know how these stress points can show up—in the form of fatigue, headaches, anxiety, overeating, fear, irritability, and many other symptoms. When they do, we really need to be mindful and take care of ourselves, *yet this is usually when we let go of self-care altogether.*

I mentioned most of our stress is manufactured by us, in our minds. (If you don't believe that, stop here for a moment. Imagine a stressful situation, such as missing a flight. Notice corresponding changes in the mind and body. Even though you just imagined this, chances are you felt some physical, emotional, or mental response to the idea of the stress of that situation.) Because most stress is created by us, *we have the power to manage how it affects us.* We will always have demands upon us; if we didn't, life might actually be pretty boring. It's how we respond to those demands that makes all the difference.

Often stress sneaks up on us when we are not mindful. We realize we don't have time to get a presentation done, for example. Our minds may start creating catastrophic outcomes, and we find we can no longer concentrate, which puts us further behind. Stress tends to beget more stress, because it wreaks havoc on our productivity, and then we're reacting to that as well. But if we are mindful and aware of our lives in each moment, we can hit an imaginary pause button when we begin to feel the effects of stress. And during that pause, we can regain perspective.

> *Between stimulus and response there is a space. In that space is our power to choose our response. In our response lies our growth and our freedom.* — *Viktor Frankl*

In summary, mindful wellness is about being present in mind, body, and spirit without letting thoughts of the past or future distract us from the moment we are in.

Each of the chapters in this book provides strategies for dealing with both sources of, and symptoms of, stress. As we become mindful, we will recognize our patterns and develop strategies for change through mindful practice.

MINDFUL PRACTICE

The following questions set the groundwork for all future mindful practices.

MINDFULNESS
1. What does being mindful mean to you?
2. Describe a recent situation in which you were not mindful. How did it feel? Did you miss anything?
3. How about a time when you felt present, complete, and in the flow? How did it feel?
4. How would being more mindful help you?

WELLNESS
1. What does wellness mean to you?
2. Describe a time in your life when you experienced wellness? What were you doing that contributed to this?

STRESS
1. What are some of your stress triggers and symptoms?
2. Are there some ways that stress has been positive for you?

AS YOU CONTINUE THROUGH THIS BOOK

In your daily life, begin to identify times when you are "in the moment." Journal about what that is like.

Mindful Intentions

Setting the stage for a new way of being

You do not need to leave your room. Remain sitting at your table and listen. Do not even listen, simply wait. The world will freely offer itself to you to be unmasked, it has no choice, it will roll in ecstasy at your feet. — Frankz Kafka

I USED TO ALWAYS MAKE New Year's resolutions. In fact, my husband, Seth, and I used to enjoy our annual ritual of going out to breakfast on the first of January and creating a list, with sections for all the usual categories: home, finances, fitness, professional, family, relationship, etc. We kept the list in a file and sometimes went back to check it to see what our progress was. We had often made great progress, with some things on the list that were right on track; but some were not, and, of course, we had completely forgotten about some of them. We would congratulate ourselves on our progress, recommit to getting on track with some things, and decide to put off other things—usually the things we had forgotten about because they were not important. So it was just fine. It made us feel good, and it certainly didn't hurt anything.

As we got busier with the kids and our jobs, writing our yearly list became sporadic, and over time we just stopped doing it. We didn't really miss it, and because we were both fairly motivated, we kept working on things that were important to us even though we didn't have a list to refer back to. These days, we don't even pretend we are going to make a list. So what changed?

Rather than resolutions, I set intentions for the year, which have less to do with what I am going to do and more to do with how I am going to approach life. For example, this year my intention is to be courageous. I still do things, of course; however, rather than starting with what I will *do,* I start with how I want to *be* in the world. If I am courageous, that sets a tone around all that I will do. It's quite motivating.

I don't have anything against New Year's resolutions, per se. Writing them could sometimes be fun, but it became less fun because I was coming to them from a place of not being "enough."

We can only control ourselves

If you come to the table with ideas of all the things you are not doing that you think you *should* be doing, making New Year's resolutions could really bum you out. Sometimes we resolve to do things that are really not in our control. Not to be a total downer, but you may resolve to get promoted in your current position and then get laid off—due to a downturn in your company's business that has nothing to do with you. We have no control over external circumstances, only over ourselves. And that's why setting intentions may be more helpful than setting goals, making resolutions, or only thinking about the finish line.

What? Did she just say we shouldn't set goals? Then how will I know how

*I am doing? This is crazy; I'm done
with this book.*

Wait, keep going. As I said, I don't really have anything against resolutions, and I think goals can be very helpful. And it's really fun to cross the finish line. However, there are more downsides to New Year's resolutions:

— The success rate is low. To understand this, go to the gym on January 5, and then go back on March 5. You'll have a lot more space to work out!

— They are all about the *shoulds*. We feel bad and guilty about our current states and need to change them by force.

— There is a focus on the negative.

— We set ourselves up for failure by being unrealistic and not taking circumstances into account.

Intentions

When we're intentional, we are determined or resolved to act in a certain way. *We have control* over how we act. So no matter what is happening around us, whether things are going our way or not, we can behave as we decide, drawing upon our will and determination to do so.

Intentions change the focus from *what* we do to *how* and *why* we do it. This leads to living intentionally.

— It's holistic. We can live in harmony with the way we want to be.

— It's more motivating and positive.

— It's more supportive and compassionate.

— It's not punitive.

"First say to yourself what you would be; then do what you have to do." – Epictetus

Intentions give us a mindful approach to life, because in each moment, we can be the way we want to be. Instead of getting distracted by the obstacles around us, we grow into having a steady and steadfast approach to our circumstances.

Here are some examples of intentions. Look at the list and see what resonates with you. Then think about what you would be able to accomplish by setting these intentions.

Intentions				
Patient	Courageous	Open-minded	Team-oriented	Strong
Mindful	Responsive	Innovative	Grateful	Free
Balanced	Responsible	Decisive	Fair	Peaceful
Leading	Compassionate	Healthy	Caring	Loving
Reliable	Memorable	Efficient	Powerful	Inspiring

> *"To action alone are we entitled, never to its fruit."*
> *– Bhagavad Gita*

So we set an intention, put our best efforts forth, and let go of the outcomes. If we continue to put our best efforts forward, we will find ourselves accomplishing more and more, and with less stress.

How to move forward with intention

✓ Take some quiet time to consider how you want to be in the world.

✓ Create some intentions based on that.

✓ Prioritize three intentions for the upcoming twelve months.

- ✓ List your tasks and goals by each intention.
- ✓ Reaffirm your intention each day before you move into your tasks.
- ✓ Enjoy how easily accomplishments come to you.

MINDFUL PRACTICE

IN THE PAST

1. Have you made New Year's resolutions in the past? How has this experience been for you?
2. How has setting goals in the past helped you? Were there any downsides to the goals you set?

TODAY

How can you affirm your intentions to yourself each day?

OVER THE MONTH

Journal about feelings, questions, and issues that have come up during this chapter about resolutions, goals, and intentions.

Mindful Breath

Your anchor to the present moment

The best and greatest is breath.
— Brihid-Aranyaka-Upanishad

BREATHING IS NOT a complicated activity. It's regulated by the autonomic nervous system, so we don't even have to think about it. Breathing is always happening, and we are usually not even aware of it. We don't have to pay attention to it, we don't have to manage it, we don't have to notice it, and it still happens. The breath is essential to life. Breath *is* life.

And, just like we have some challenges in life, we often have challenges with our breath—with the act of breathing, itself. We experience stress and we hold our breath—hold our emotions or reactions in the body. This disrupts the flows in our bodies—not just the flow of respiration, but also of digestion. It causes stress on the body as systems look out for what to do in the absence of healthy breathing.

> Breathing is one of the simplest things in the world. We breathe in, we breathe out. When we breathe with real freedom, we neither grasp for nor hold on to the breath. No effort is required to pull the breath in or push the breath out. Given the simplicity of breathing one would think it was the easiest thing to do in the world. However, if it were truly so easy there would be few unhappy or unhealthy people in the world. To become a welcome vessel for the breath is to live life without trying to control, grasp, or push away. And how easy is this? The process of breathing is the most accurate metaphor we have for the way that we personally approach life, how we live our lives, and how we react to the inevitable changes that life brings us.
>
> — Donna Farhi, *The Breathing Book: Good Health and Vitality through Essential Breath Work*

The breath is in real time

I often teach Yoga movements as being initiated by each breath. Each happens right now, in every

moment, so it is a good anchor to the present
moment. If we hold our breath, we are keeping
ourselves away from the present moment. In Yoga, a
breath is associated with the movement of prana,
which means life force or animating force. That
seems like something we would like to keep flowing,
yes?

A breath can return us to the present moment time
and time again, because It is always happening. It
happens in real time, right now. A breath can connect
the mind and body and give a feeling of overall well-
being—one of the many reasons why people join a
Yoga class. Yet it is quite common that in the middle
of class, when we are moving into a more challenging
portion of the practice, I feel this sense of complete
suspense, and I realize that no one seems to be
breathing! Often, all the participants are
subconsciously holding their breath to get through
some difficulty in the practice. Or they are
concentrating so hard, they forget to breathe for a
moment. Or they think that by holding a breath, they
won't move, and therefore it will be easier to balance.
As soon as I realize this, I will ask if anyone is holding
his or her breath, only to be met with a variety of
sounds that happen when one stops holding one's

breath. This usually gets everyone laughing sheepishly. However, as students create a consistent practice, this will happen less and less often.

The benefits of breathing deeply

Deep breathing calms the nervous system. Here are some other cool things about taking full, deep breaths:

— It lowers blood pressure.

— It strengthens the abdominals.

— It promotes blood flow.

— It releases toxins.

— It promotes deep sleep.

— Endorphins are released, promoting feelings of well-being and pain-reduction.

Each of our breaths can also be a practice of balance—an equal exchange of what we bring in and what we let go of.

I took a deep breath and listened to that old bray of my heart: I am, I am, I am. — Sylvia Plath

The downside to poor breathing techniques

Breathing is natural; however, due to tension, stress, and conditioning, we may not be breathing in a way that nourishes us. In the very moments when it would really be nice to calm down, we create more stress to the system by allowing our muscles to tense and restrict our breathing.

You may not actually hold your breath when facing something difficult, but your breath may become shallower, again prohibiting a deep relaxation response. In addition to breath holding and shallow breathing, many people have other dysfunctional breathing habits. Unhealthy breathing both causes, and is a reaction to, stress. It inhibits our wellness because we lose the peace within our grasp in each moment.

With normal breathing, the inhalation brings breath into the body, filling it up like a balloon, and the exhalation causes the body to contract around the center as the breath leaves the body. However, there are many people who will squeeze their bellies as they inhale (reverse breathing), resulting in a lack of oxygen to the body; then they will expand the belly on the exhale, which doesn't necessarily allow for a full exhalation. While reverse breathing is actually a technique sometimes used in Qigong and some other practices, it is not helpful for the average person who does so without even knowing it.

> Every breath can be a practice. With the inhalation, imagine drawing in pure, cleansing, relaxing energies. And with each exhalation, imagine expelling all obstacles, stress, and negative emotions. This is not something that requires a particular place in which to sit. It can be done when in the car on the way to work, waiting for a stop light, sitting in front of the computer, preparing a meal, cleaning the house, or walking.
> — Tenzin Wangyal Rinpoche, *The Tibetan Yogas of Dream and Sleep*

Breathing check-in

1. Lie down on your back and get comfortable.
2. Without trying to change anything, be aware of each breath you take. As you get accustomed to the rhythm of each breath, start to follow it by staying aware.
3. Place one hand over your heart and one hand over your belly.

4. On the inhalation, as the body fills with the breath, the hands will be gently raised by the body.

On the exhalation, as the body empties of the breath, the hands will gently move downward.

Don't force the hands to go up or down, simply ride the wave of the breath.

5. If you notice that your hands sink down on the *inhalation,* you may be doing reverse breathing. Pause, and on the next inhalation, gently press the

hands up with the breath and release the hands down when you exhale.

6. You may also notice that you run out of breath before the hand that is on your belly has a chance to ride up with the breath. Over time, and with practice, you will find that the breath reaches farther down to expand the belly as well. Here are a few more to try:

Three-part breathing

This is a basic practice to deepen the breath. It can be used any time you need to slow down, regain perspective, find focus, or just get a grip.

Sit on the floor or in a chair. When you inhale, draw the breath in through the nose and feel it lift your heart, open your ribs, and then stretch your belly. When you exhale, feel the belly relax, feel the ribs hug around you, and feel the heart melt toward the spine, even as you sit nice and tall. Repeat, allowing the breath to be fluid, each "part" flowing into the next, and simply be aware of how the breath moves in the body.

Alternate nostril breathing to balance your energy

In Yoga philosophy, the right side of the body is associated with sun, or Surya energy, which is activating, energizing, and heating; and the left side of the body is associated with moon, or Chandra energy, which is nurturing, calming, and cooling. So when we breathe in and out through the right nostril, we can create more heating active energy, and when we breathe in and out through the left nostril, we can create more calming energy.

At any given moment, one nostril dominates, which can also influence the energy. In this breath technique—called alternate nostril breathing, or *nadhi shodhana*—we direct the breath through the nostrils to bring energy up, down, or into balance. This is a very simple explanation of a practice that can become very nuanced with more study and practice.

When you want to bring the energy up:
Sit on the floor or in a chair. Using your right hand, gently curl your fingers and close your left nostril with your ring finger. You can rest other fingers on the forehead or just leave them curled. Breathe in and out through the right nostril. Begin with one minute, breathing at a natural pace, and increase the amount of time.

When you want to bring the energy down or calm yourself:
You will do the same thing, using the thumb to close off the right nostril as you breathe in and out through the left nostril.

To bring yourself into balance:
Use your right hand and close your right nostril with the thumb. Breathe in through the left nostril. Close the left nostril with the ring finger and breathe out through the right nostril. Breathe in through the right nostril and close the right nostril with the thumb as you release the left nostril. Breathe out through the left nostril and then back in through the

left nostril. Move from side to side in this way, beginning with one minute and adding more time as you are ready.

These are but a few ways to practice healthy breathing patterns. Many breath practices can help you feel mindful and well during the day. Learning to deepen the breath consciously can help you feel calm and whole. Healthy breaths really are a cornerstone to *mindful wellness.*

> We spend most of our time caught up in the memories of the past or looking ahead to the future, full of worries and plans. The breath has none of that "other-timeness." When we truly observe the breath, we are automatically placed in the present. We are pulled out of the morass of mental images and into a bare experience of the here-and-now. In this sense, breath is a living slice of reality. A mindful observation of such a miniature model of life itself leads to insights that are broadly applicable to the rest of our experience.
> — Henepola Gunaratana, *Beyond Mindfulness in Plain English: An Introductory Guide to Deeper States of Meditation*

How to move forward with the breath

✓ Take some time to pay attention to your breaths. This might be first thing in the morning or in the evening before you go to bed. Spend 1–5 minutes tuning in to your breaths.

✓ Practice these breathing techniques daily.

MINDFUL PRACTICE

1. Notice how your breathing patterns change during the day.
   a. What happens when you are under stress?
   b. What happens when you are tired?
   c. What happens when you are energized?
   d. How does your breathing change with your mood?
   e. How does your mood change with your breaths?
2. During your day, stop and take three deep breaths. How do you feel?
3. During the day, notice which nostril is dominant. Can you track that to how your energy is flowing?

*For videos of the breathing exercises in this chapter, and much more, visit my website: www.beingwellyoga.com/breathpractice

Mindful Movement

Yoga as a path to awareness

The rhythm of the body, the melody
of the mind and the harmony of the
soul create the symphony of life.
— BKS Iyengar

HOW DO I EXPLAIN a 5,000-year-old Indian body of knowledge in one chapter? The task feels daunting, but I start to dig in by looking outward; I do some research to see how others have distilled this vast topic. I don't know how to condense it into a short explanation, and I begin to doubt myself—I judge myself and my experience as inadequate to do the topic of Yoga justice. But then I look inward at what I can tap into—what my Yoga practice has taught me over the years—and I get a handle on myself for the task at hand.

Yoga is so much more than exercise

Many people think that Yoga is about creating pretzel-like shapes with the body or performing inconceivable acts of balance, but true Yoga is about so much more than getting flexible and doing Down Dog—the most famous of the Yoga postures in the United States.

The word Yoga comes from the Sanskrit *Yuj*, which means to join or yoke. Think of Yoga as bringing things together in harmony. The practice of Yoga is about being more connected. You might think of this as connecting the mind and the body, connecting us to our inner selves, or feeling connected to the universe.

The physical practice of Yoga is only one of eight limbs or stages of Yoga, as described in the *Yoga Sutras of Pantanjali,* the primary text of raja Yoga. The others deal with how we interact with ourselves and the world around us, the control of our senses and breathing, our ability to concentrate and meditate, and enlightenment.

While the Yoga sutras consist of a total of 196 sutras or "threads," this second sutra about controlling one's thoughts is the one that is most significant for me:

> *"Yoga chitta vritti nirodhah—Yoga is the restraint of the modifications of the mind."*
> — *Sutra 1.2 of the Yoga Sutras of Patanjali*

— The modifications of the mind are our thoughts.
— Yoga is the restraint of our thoughts. So Yoga allows us to get control of our thoughts so they don't control us.

Muddling our minds

We are so busy all the time. With all that we do, the mind gets very busy and cluttered. We often get lost in our thoughts or let them run away with us. Worse, we begin to identify with our busyness, roles, activities, and thoughts.

Our thoughts are sometimes based on facts and grounded in reality, but not always. Sometimes they are a complete fabrication, conjured up by our beliefs and conditioning.

Don't believe everything you think.

Of course, we do need to have thoughts; they are really quite helpful tools. Yet imagine a life without overthinking and the possibilities that might open up. If we can just put a little perspective between our true selves and our thoughts, we can really live in each moment rather than dredge up the past or project out into the future.

We need to practice letting go of the thoughts that pursue us day and night. If we can, we will find that all the busyness in the ever-active monkey-mind was obscuring our true nature—our deeper understanding of who we are versus what we do. Just as with intention-setting, who and how we *are* is more important than what we do. Yoga helps us practice clearing our minds by detaching from our thoughts.

> *You are the sky. Everything else is just the weather.*
> — *Pema Chödrön*

In a physical Yoga class, we use movement as a tool to practice mindfulness. I explain to new students that Yoga is different from other activities we engage in because we ask that the mind take a back seat in the experience. And in this way, Yoga can be a path to mindfulness. We experience each movement rather than think about it. Over time we develop a sense of the body and its alignment and healthy movement patterns. We build strength where we need support, nurture flexibility where we are rigid, and bring balance into the body. We cultivate comfort and ease in both the body and the mind. Our practice gives us the felt sense or experience that enables us to access that comfort and ease, regardless of the circumstances surrounding us. This can serve us as we remain calm and centered in the midst of a crisis.

Further, finding comfort, ease, and balance in the body can help us to be mindful and remain fully in the moment, because we do not have aches and pains distracting us.

> *Peace. It does not mean to be in a place where there is no noise, trouble, or hard work. It means to be in the midst of those things and still be calm in your heart.*
> *— Unknown*

Your Yoga practices

There are many ways to practice Yoga. You might read an article about a few Yoga postures or asanas and begin to do those at home. Maybe it's a Yoga video, or a public or private session with an experienced teacher. There are Yoga retreats, Yoga meetups, and Yoga hikes. Dogs and cats do Yoga these days, and baby goats are even involved in some Yoga classes. It's not really important what you do in Yoga; it's how and why you do it.

In order to make your physical practice a true practice in mindfulness, set aside some dedicated time for it every day. This begins the mindfulness practice and creates a deliberate space for you. It also reinforces that you have made a commitment to yourself. It's good to decide how you want to move through your practice in advance. Ask yourself, *Why am I here practicing today?* There may be something you want to cultivate, such as patience, perspective, presence, or compassion. There may be something you want to let go of, such as anger, control, or a habit that doesn't serve you. You may wish to send your efforts out in honor of something or someone bigger than yourself, such as dedicating your practice to peace in the world. This will guide you through, and, no matter what you do physically in the practice, you will honor your intention and it can nourish you.

Another roadblock can be your expectation as to how you're doing as you move through your practice, so do not judge your efforts; just experience them. Allow the experience to unfold, practicing being present for the experience. As judgments and expectations arise, you have the opportunity to observe them dispassionately as you practice regaining perspective about your thoughts.

If you scan your body and mind to see what you are carrying with you in the moment, you can become aware of what you need to let go of. As you move through your life, your body and mind are constantly organizing and reorganizing to deal with everything you come in contact with so that you can effectively manage whatever comes your way. And once you have made it through the situation, there is still a residue or remainder with you. It could be a sensation in the body, a thought, an energy, or an emotion. This is why you need to observe what is with you in the moment as you begin to practice. If you don't pay attention on an ongoing basis, there may be something much bigger to notice in future practices, such as an illness or injury.

The breath is a fantastic anchor to the present moment. When you tune into the rhythm of each breath, as I previously discussed, your breath can also provide feedback on your practice and tell you whether you are overdoing or underdoing it, and whether or not you are really present.

Find your edge in your practice—the place where your breath and body tell you to stop. The edge is where you know you are making some change—you feel the feedback in the body—some stretching, strengthening, stability, or balance is being challenged, but you are not pushing so much that you are getting hurt. A good way to think about the edge is that it is a place where you could stay for a while without getting hurt, but you might not necessarily want to stay there. Sometimes when we get to the edge in a posture, there is more sensation than we want to deal with and it feels quite challenging or uncomfortable. It is easy to distract ourselves so we don't have to experience the discomfort fully; however, don't look away. The practice of finding this union with ourselves requires that we look deeply into the sensation, no matter how difficult. We learn to distinguish the discomfort from pain. No change comes without some level of discomfort—the more we can face it, the more we can be fully in our lives as participants, not observers. This practice helps us to live *in* our lives rather than just living *out* our lives.

Self-compassion in practice

Cultivate compassion for yourself in practice. Your practice allows you to truly observe and listen to yourself without judgment. Once you find that compassion, you create a container of acceptance of yourself exactly as you are, and you deal with things as they come up rather than ignore or resist them. When you honestly and compassionately accept what is and face it, you can begin to move through these issues to create change.

Notice when the thinking mind starts to assert itself. We have so many conditioned habits and practices. We have habits in the way that we communicate with ourselves, and we are often attached to the way we think about things. In your practice, as you become conscious of your patterns and attachments, you can release your hold on them.

At the end of the practice, rest fully to integrate the work you have done in practice. The final posture in a Yoga class is called svasana, and it means corpse pose. It symbolizes the ultimate point in letting go of your attachments. You rest quietly, allowing yourself to *be* rather than *do.* This is often the most challenging part of the physical Yoga practice, at least initially. Once you allow yourself this deep rest, it may actually become your favorite part.

Your Yoga practices will help you to be mindful in your everyday life, and when you are, you can be more effective at everything you do.

Yoga practice

Beginning on the next page is a short practice you can try at home.

> Follow your nature. The practice is really about uncovering your own pose; we have great respect for our teachers, but unless we can uncover our own pose in the moment, it's not practice — it's mimicry. Rest deeply in Savasana every day. Always enter that pratyahara (withdrawn state) every day. And just enjoy yourself. For many years I mistook discipline as ambition. Now I believe it to be more about consistency. Do get on the mat. Practice and life are not that different.
>
> – Judith Hanson Lasater, "Judith Hanson Lasater, PhD," www.yogajournal.com blog

SUKASANA/SEATED CENTERING – Sit on the floor in a crossed-legged position. If your hips, back, or shoulders feel tight, place a blanket or pillow underneath the hips.

Spend a few moments here just checking in with yourself and noticing how you are feeling. You can place the hands together or leave them resting on your legs.

MARAJIASANA-BITILASANA/CAT/COW –

Come into a tabletop position with the hands under the shoulders and the knees under the hips. Inhale, and lift your heart as you lengthen the tailbone. Exhale, drop the head, arch your back like a cat, and tuck your tailbone under. Repeat 3–8 times.

SALAMBA BHUJANGASANA/SPHINX – Rest,
face down, on your belly. Bring your elbows under
your shoulders and prop your upper body up like a
sphinx. Press the tops of your toes into the mat, lift
your heart, and lengthen the back of the neck. Hold
for several breaths. Rest on your belly for a few
breaths.

SUPTA PARIVARTANASANA/TWIST – Lie on your back. Let your arms stretch out from your shoulders. Gently drop the knees to the right, supporting them with a block or blankets. Stay for a few breaths and then switch to the other side. Repeat 2–3 times. If you feel irritation in the back, move your hips two inches in the opposite direction before dropping your knees (e.g., If you are dropping the knees to the right, move your hips a couple of inches to the left before you do that).

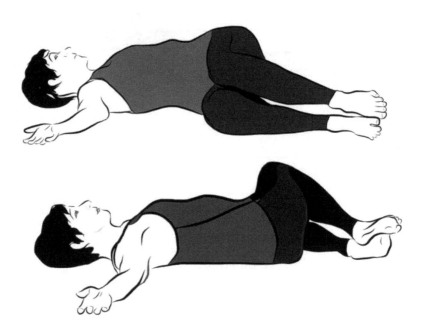

UTTANASANA/STANDING FORWARD
FOLD – Stand up with feet about hip distance apart.
Gently bend your knees and walk your hands down
your legs until you feel a stretch in the legs. Keep the
weight even between the front and back of the foot.
Don't overstrain trying to reach for your toes, or
hyperextend the legs; the idea is to get a good stretch
in the back of the body. You can place your hands on
a block if you choose. Stay for a breath or two and
come up slowly. Repeat 2–3 times.

VIRABHADRASANA 2/WARRIOR 2 – Stand in a straddle position. Turn your right toes to the right and bend your right knee so that it is over the right ankle and tracking over the middle toes. Extend your arms from your shoulder and look over the right fingertips. Stay for several breaths and then do this on the other side. Repeat 2–3 times.

JANU SIRSASANA/HEAD TO KNEE POSE –

Sit on the floor or on a blanket and bring your legs out in front of you. Bend your right knee and open it up to the right, letting the hip rotate to allow for this. Place the right foot against the left leg. You may want to support your right knee by placing a block underneath it. Gently fold the body over the left leg. Take 3–8 breaths and repeat on the other side. As you continue to practice, feel free to extend the amount of time you hold the posture.

DWIPADA PITHAM/BRIDGE – Lie on your back with the knees bent and the feet about hip distance apart, arms by your sides. Gently lengthen and lift the tailbone off the mat; and continue to lift the back body up until you are supported by your feet, arms, shoulders, and the back of the head. Take a breath or two here and return the back body to the mat. You might also consider placing a block under your sacrum for support as you build strength in your back body. Repeat 2–3 times.

PRANYAMA/BREATH WORK – Choose any of the breath techniques from the previous chapter.

SVASANA/REST – Make sure you don't shortchange this one. It's vitally important to the integration of mindful body awareness. It can be hard for some people who are used to being busy, because in this posture we don't do anything. Simply lie on your back and make yourself comfortable. This may mean putting a rolled blanket under your knees or a blanket under your head. Try to keep a comfortable, natural curve of the spine. Let your arms rest by your sides and let your legs relax and gently roll open. Close your eyes and just allow yourself to let go. Stay here for as much time as you have. If you don't want to worry about the time, set a timer that will chime when it is time to get up. Get up slowly and sit still for a few moments before you get up and go into your day.

How to move forward with Yoga

- ✓ Set aside some dedicated time for your practice.
- ✓ Set an intention for your practice.
- ✓ Commit to letting go of judgment and expectation.
- ✓ Scan the body and the mind to see what you are carrying with you in the moment.
- ✓ Tune into the rhythm of each breath.
- ✓ Find your edge in your practice.
- ✓ Don't look away.
- ✓ Cultivate compassion for yourself in practice.
- ✓ Notice when the thinking mind starts to assert itself.

At the end of the practice, rest fully to integrate the work that you have done in practice. Then journal about your experience.

MINDFUL PRACTICE

Create your practice plan.

1. How many days will you practice?
2. For how long?
3. Where?
4. What do you need to do to clear space in your schedule to practice?
5. Choose a few postures to begin with. Over time, you will become very intuitive and move through postures that feel helpful in the moment.

*For videos of the short daily practice in this chapter, and much more, visit my website: www.beingwellyoga.com/yogapractice

Mindful Energy Management

Go with the flow and take time to recharge

*Yoga means addition – addition of
energy, strength and beauty to
body, mind and soul. — Amit Ray*

I AM A MORNING PERSON, and have been for about the past twenty years. I spring out of bed at a very early hour, no snooze button needed, and I am on my way. I don't even consider going back to bed. I like to get my workout done in the morning, and I enjoy the quiet time before the rest of the world wakes up. It helps to set up a mindful day, because I get to pay attention to how I feel and what is going on with me *before* I head out into the world. I get most of my work and Yoga classes completed before 3 p.m. Lucky for me/us, Seth thrives on an early-to-bed, early-to-rise schedule as well. It works for us. I know that I feel most energetic early in the day and run out of steam early in the evening, so I don't try to fight it. I work with my energy nature.

It's essential to understand your energy nature and work with it rather than against it. When people ask me about my teaching schedule, they often say, "Oh, I wish I could get up that early! Someday I will surprise you and show up in your early morning class." They never do, and that's fine; each of us has a rhythm, and we should honor that. Paying attention to that is a great aspect of *mindful wellness.*

You may feel, as your energy ebbs and flows, that you don't have any control over whether you are wound up or lethargic. The truth is there are lots of ways you can help yourself sustain your energy and feel more balanced throughout the day. The great thing about energy is that it is a renewable resource, so you can be much better off managing your energy than trying to manage time—which, rather than being renewable, just keeps ticking away.

It's helpful to be mindful of which of the following leave you feeling drained or refreshed in an average day:
- — Activities and time spent on tasks
- — People
- — Amount of sleep
- — Use of stimulants and depressants like coffee and alcohol
- — Balanced meals
- — Exercise

Activities, tasks, and rest periods

No one is fully energized 100 percent during the day. We all have ultradian rhythms to our days and nights—rest or activity cycles. Research shows that the brain can focus for one and a half to two hours, after which we lose momentum, motivation, and productivity; unless the activity or task energizes us and we can go for longer. We often just keep barreling through until we get the next cycle of energy, but if we are not taking a rest cycle, we become less and less productive through the day. Recognizing these cycles can help us manage energy throughout the day.

Breaking up tasks into ninety-minute portions can help us manage our energy and be more productive. Given too much time to do a task, we can tend to fritter the time away and get nothing done. However, if we set a timer and get to work for ninety minutes at a time, we can usually get much more accomplished.

A recommended rest cycle of about twenty minutes is ideal for clearing the mind and reenergizing before beginning your next task.

Draining tasks

When I have to go over business accounting with my bookkeeper, I feel completely drained of energy—it's the type of task that I dread. For her, on the other hand, it's fun and motivating to help people keep their books.

We all have tasks that we don't like to do as much as others. If you have draining tasks in your day, try scheduling them so that there are renewing tasks in-between. Or perhaps you hate a certain weekly meeting you have to attend. Explore whether it is really necessary weekly—can it be shorter, or is there another way to do it?

If you are only involved in tasks and activities that deplete you, it's time to take a deeper dive into that and see what changes you need to make in your day so that you feel more alive. Make changes to maximize activity that nourish and energize you.

People

There are people who fill you with positive energy and others who totally zap you of all energy. Surround yourself with people who bring you energy and with whom you feel an equal energy exchange.

We all have the one person who sucks energy out of us and then goes on with his or her day. What is it about the relationship that is leading to that? Can you make some changes? You may not need to have so much interaction with that person. If that person is a coworker or family member, you may not have the choice to disengage. In that case, you may need to reevaluate your expectations of the person, develop some strategies for coping, and change your perspective through reframing. If the person talks incessantly, you can kindly let him or her know that you have other time commitments. If you do have time to listen, reframe by allowing yourself to admire the wealth of information he or she is sharing. We can't change other people; we can only elevate our mindful approach to better manage our interactions.

Sleep

Get enough sleep. Most healthy adults need between seven and nine hours of sleep each night. Most people don't get enough. You may not even know what it feels like to be rested. You might not be getting enough sleep if you fall asleep watching TV, or in Yoga class, or during a presentation or class, or at your desk. You may think everyone does that, and many people do.

You possibly will not be getting enough sleep because you are not sleepy at night, and then you get a second wind and stay up really late. Then the alarm goes off and you push yourself out of bed, even though you don't feel rested. You try to catch up on sleep over the weekend, then start the cycle again. Or you are too stressed, anxious, or wound up to get to sleep at a reasonable hour. In our plugged-in, stressed-out world, this is quite common. Sometimes you're looking at a digital screen right up to bedtime.

Here are some ways to get more sleep:

— You have probably heard that it is helpful to shut off all screens an hour before you go to bed, and it is. If the ten o'clock news is the last thing you see before you try to nod off, it's going to be a challenge!

— Think about an evening routine or ritual—this will be covered more in-depth in month 6. Slowing down, reading a book, taking a warm bath, or meditating may set the stage for a better night's sleep.

— Have a bedtime. My phone has a feature called "bedtime." I put in the time that I want to wake up, how long I want to sleep, and it then gives me a bedtime based on that. Fifteen minutes before bedtime, my phone vibrates, reminding me to start getting ready for bed.

Ups and downs with coffee and alcohol

Use caffeine and alcohol mindfully. The coffee cycle begins when you wake up tired and need that jolt of caffeine to get going, then maybe a cup of coffee in the afternoon to keep going, and probably several more. Depending on how your body metabolizes caffeine, this could be affecting your sleep.

Several years ago, I was at a Yoga retreat where no coffee was available. I was only a one-cup-a-day girl, but I still had a withdrawal headache for those days. I decided, once the retreat was over, to let go of the caffeine and switch to decaf. I like the taste, the warmth, and the ritual of a morning coffee. Within days I noticed I was sleeping better, even though I wasn't drinking much coffee to begin with! And the great thing about being a decaf drinker is that I don't "need" my morning coffee—if I have it, great, but if it's not available, my body doesn't care.

Alcohol affects each of us differently. It is a depressant, so it can make you feel sleepy and perhaps fall asleep quickly. However, overindulging will lead to interrupted sleep and dehydration later in the night, which can affect your energy as well.

Balanced meals

I'll talk much more in depth about nutrition in month 7, but when thinking of energy balance, I have to at least mention food. Staying well-nourished and hydrated gives you the fuel to keep working through your day—feeding the body and the mind. Starving yourself early in the day may make it hard to focus on tasks. If you drink coffee rather than eat, you might get jittery and need to bring the energy down so you can focus. Heavy foods can also make you tired—the body needs to work very hard to digest heavier foods, and this takes its toll.

Over or undereating will certainly affect your energy. Your body needs fuel throughout the day. If you don't eat enough at lunch, chances are you will feel that three o'clock energy lull. If you overeat, your body will be so busy figuring out how to digest it all that you will also feel that mid-afternoon energy slump at three o'clock.

Sugar can also wreak havoc on your energy balance, spiking energy when you reach for that candy bar and then dumping you into a tired heap when the energy plummets. Eating balanced meals that have carbohydrates, fats, and protein will keep your body balanced throughout the day.

Exercise

A regular exercise plan can help you to balance your energy. Your morning workout may leave you feeling up and ready for the day, or maybe a midday exercise break is best for you. A brisk walk around the office or block can reenergize you in the middle of the day— try that instead of a Snickers bar when you need a little oomph. Some let off stress and anxiety through an evening workout, although exercising too late at night may interfere with getting to sleep at a reasonable hour, so just be mindful of that.

If you are too tired to even think about starting an exercise program, start very small. You don't need an entire workout to begin; just get up and take a short walk. Each day, add a little to that, and before long you may have found your reenergizing workout plan.

Keep an energy journal in which you include the ebbs and flows of energy in your day, as well as your sleep patterns.

One-minute resets to manage your energy

- ✓ Deep breaths. Take three deep breaths and then pause. You will notice an immediate shift toward balance.
- ✓ Long inhalations and exhalations. If you are feeling sluggish, take a few breaths and let the inhalations be a little longer than the exhalations. If you are feeling wound up or anxious, take a few breaths and let the exhalations be a little longer than the inhalations.
- ✓ Stop multi-tasking. Do one thing at a time and focus on what you are doing.
- ✓ Stand up and stretch.
- ✓ Drink a glass of water.

- ✓ Change your perspective. Ask yourself, how else can I look at this? Make a mental list of five things you are grateful for.
- ✓ Call a friend who uplifts you.
- ✓ Breathe in some peppermint or citrus scent to energize you. Breathe in some lavender or vanilla to relax you.

MINDFUL PRACTICE

1. Are you a night person or a morning person, or a little of each? How does this affect your energy each day?
2. Think about the flow of energy during the day. Where are the peaks and where are the lulls? What is the best time for productive work for you?
3. What are your biggest energy challenges? Using ideas from this chapter, create a turnaround plan for each.

Mindful Media Detox

Connections that enhance your life

"Be present to the people in front of you from moment to moment. Electronics and technology have a way of clouding our vision for the people sitting next to us. Uncloud your life, look around. Be present."

— Eric Overby, Journey

HOW CAN WE STAY MINDFUL in this digital age? Theoretically, we should have lots more time, as some tasks we used to do are managed by our smart phones. But that's not what seems to be happening.

This chapter invites you to mindfully look at how you operate in the digital world in relation to your productivity, well-being, and presence.

The average American adult spends *about ten and a half hours a day* staring at a screen of some kind, and that number is growing. While some screens, such as TV screens, have been part of the landscape for a long time, the proliferation of screens is a fairly new phenomenon.

It's not news to any of us that technology has given us a lot more options and abilities, making many things in our lives feel easier. I love spending five minutes online to order a product and have it show up on my doorstep the next day, or sometimes even in the next hour, instead of spending time doing errands I don't find very fulfilling. And yet...

I was headed out on a ten-hour road trip recently. To prepare, I had loaded my phone with podcasts and music. I had phone numbers programmed in my phone so I could catch up on phone calls and *make the time productive.* My phone had the route already set and was ready to alert me when it was time to make a turn or exit. I was driving my son's car and plugged in the charger that was there to connect my phone ... and my screen went black and my phone died instantly. So there I was, just me in the car for ten hours without my podcasts and music and phone numbers. I was forced to just do the thing I was doing—drive for ten hours. And so I did.

I looked for distraction via FM radio, yet there were long stretches without reception. I got to actually experience what I was doing. I felt the road under my tires and heard the rush of other cars. I noticed the clear blue of the sky—it was a gorgeous day. I saw and felt the character of the small towns I passed through, and even got to investigate my feelings, assumptions, and judgments about them. I noticed formations of birds, shapes of clouds, and dense forests flanking the highway. I noticed, and accepted, my impatience and my frustration—when I saw a sign that indicated I had more time left to drive than I'd thought.

I arrived at my destination and the experience ended. Like most things, it had been temporary. I decided to reflect on the lessons, which I am still doing. I had two more days before my phone (with one week left on its warranty—a miracle) was replaced. I knew I was missing calls and texts, but I realized that most of those were distractions and that

I could mindfully decide who I truly needed to communicate with. And I decided to surrender.

Most things are not as urgent as we think—we just create more distraction by crafting a story about how important everything is, how involved we need to be, and how busy we are. I am very busy, and I know that some of that busyness is of my own creation and not truly necessary.

According to Pew Research, about 95 percent of Americans have a cell phone.

The average person checks his or her cell phone 110 times a day and spends over four hours a day on it.

— 40 percent of people use their cell phone on the toilet.

— 61 percent of people, including me, keep their cell phones under their pillows or next to the bed.

— 50 percent of people feel uneasy if they go out and leave their cell phones at home.[1]

And these numbers don't include computer and TV screen time.

Watch your thoughts; they become words. Watch your words, they become actions. Watch your actions, they

become habits. Watch your habits, they become your
character. Watch your character, it becomes your
destiny. — Lao Tzu

Productivity

Multitasking

The average person is getting almost seven hours of sleep each night, and those hours seem to be the only time we are not interacting with technology. This means that we are doing a lot of things while we are staring at screens—eating, bathing, exercising, going out to restaurants, etc. I'm not here to get into a debate on whether or not cell phones belong in the classroom (they might), or at the dinner table (they don't), or on the bedside table (probably not the best).

Multitasking is actually not. I have friends who pride themselves in their ability to do several tasks simultaneously. When I multitask, I find that I am not doing any of the multiple tasks at all. If you are splitting your attention, it is impossible to be mindful. Even reading a magazine while watching TV limits your ability to digest information from either one. If you are talking on the phone while reading an e-mail, something is going to slip by you. Mistakes get made and things have to be redone. Multitasking often leads to redoing and reworking.

Our numerous screens make it easy to multitask, and they even make us feel like we are missing out on a lot if we don't do everything at once. Texts and alerts feel urgent, and our intentions can fly out the window if we pay attention to the distractions.

Instead of multitasking, try doing just one thing at a time. You may have to put down your phone for that. If it feels weird to put down your phone, it is definitely time to take a look at your digital media and screen habits and attachments.

Staying unfocused
We develop a habit of distraction. Rather than getting to the task at hand, we look for distractions. This gives us the impression that we are doing things—answering e-mails and texts, looking up things, and managing information. But we are really just managing distractions that take us away from our true intentions.

Productivity derailed
Our ability to concentrate and get things done is compromised. When someone interrupts you at work, it can take up to twenty-three minutes to

refocus on the previous task. And we are interrupted constantly with alerts from our devices. If you feel like you don't have enough hours in the day, it may be that your device is derailing your productivity.

Well-being

Too much screen time can affect our well-being and health in many ways.

Deteriorating eyesight

Eyestrain is a common issue for those spending too much time with the screen. Further, the blue light emitted from screens can be damaging to our retinas.

Not enough exercise

A sedentary lifestyle can lead to lots of health issues. You could argue that cell phones don't make you more sedentary because you use them on the go, but we know that more screen time keeps us from moving. This could be working on computer, a text-fest on your phone, binge-watching Netflix, or playing video games. We sit down to unwind with a video game and are surprised that three hours have passed and we didn't get to work out or go to bed on time. A sedentary lifestyle is associated with obesity, heart issues, weakness in the body, and depression.

Interrupted sleep schedules or lack of sleep
We watch a show on TV to relax and end up watching five episodes. Using screens up until we go to bed can keep us from falling asleep and from getting a good night's sleep.

Restructuring of the brain
According to *Psychology Today*, a large amount of screen time leads to a restructuring of gray matter in the brain, which impacts the white matter in the brain and can lead to general poor cognitive performance.[2] Ever feel dazed after a long screen session?

Tech addiction
When the brain thinks we are getting a reward, we feel the positive effects of dopamine. Every alert from our candy-colored screens is a potential reward, making it ever harder to step away. When we become addicted, it can take us out of our lives, out of our bodies, and even make us feel like we are out of our minds.

Stress
I don't actually feel like I have more time now that I have a smart phone. I find that I can often be just as busy and stressed as ever, and often more so, because

the portability of the screens brings work into my home, social pressures into my vacations, and a constant barrage of information and e-mails that feels like a burden at all hours.

Being present

When we are just watching rather than experiencing life, we lose some of our ability to relate, empathize, and communicate. We lose our ability to just be. We put the phone on the nightstand so we will wake up to the alarm and then create a habit of checking our phones before we brush our teeth, walk the dog, or contemplate our intention for the day. We forget what it is like to watch TV without working on our computers. It becomes a cycle; we are afraid to be disconnected even for a few minutes, to the point where we start to lose our ability to process emotion. Part of the reason why we do it is because we are afraid of missing out on something if we don't.

We keep the phone handy in case the babysitter calls and end up checking texts during a dinner out, rather than paying attention to the person physically present with us, and relationships suffer.

One of the reasons I love being in the Yoga studio, whether to take a class or to teach one, is that it is a cell phone-free zone. I actually have seen people checking their phones during svasana, but it is rare. I don't even think about my phone during class, and doing Yoga is when I feel the most present, calm, and connected. How can we create that same sense at other times in our lives?

Technology is an unbelievable tool. As I said, it makes our lives easier in many ways. However, bad tech habits sneak up on us without our really noticing.

How to move forward toward mindful connections

- ✓ Set your intention first each morning. Schedule times to check your phone and respond. Let people know you won't respond immediately anymore.
- ✓ Meditate. This practice helps to restructure the brain in a positive way, enhancing concentration, calmness, and creativity.
- ✓ Get outside. Take a walk and notice your surroundings. Meet your neighbors, pet a dog, feel the earth underneath your feet.

✓ Stop trying to multitask. When you do something, do that one thing and give it your full attention.
✓ Limit your screen time and turn off all screens an hour before you go to bed.

It's not easy to break the habits of constant digital connection, but I challenge you to try. Become aware of how much time you spend in front of screens. Once you are aware, you can find opportunities to unplug a little bit and journal about the changes.

MINDFUL PRACTICE

1. How much time are you spending in front of screens? Does it help or hinder your day?
2. How many enjoyable things would you get done instead that you wish you had time to do?
3. When is your screen time not serving you? If you gave those times up, is there something you can reward yourself with by using the extra time for other activities?

Mindful Mornings and Evenings

Daily habits to support your well-being

*The ritual of our daily lives
permeates our very bodies.*
— Banana Yoshimoto

I LOVE TO LEAD YOGA RETREATS. The flow of the day is truly beautiful. Typically, we will wake up with the sun, practice Yoga, eat breakfast, and have free time or activities. Then we close the day with more Yoga, dinner, and an after-dinner check-in for the group with a meditation. We sleep soon after sundown.

The rising and setting of the sun creates a perfect container for the day, and it is easy to fall into a mindful rhythm when we start and end our day with the flow of nature. The morning Yoga practice sets us up for the day, connecting us to ourselves, our intentions, each other, and the place where we are. The evening practice helps us to integrate the day's activities, wind down, and reconnect with ourselves. If it sounds pretty idyllic, it is. Because we are on a retreat, it is easy to take the time for these morning and evening rituals—it's a big part of why we retreat; yet, it is possible to bring some rituals into our day-to-day lives as well.

How do you start your day? Do you wake up ready to go, or do you hit the snooze button? Do you grab your phone or turn on the TV? Pour yourself some coffee? And how about the end of the day? How do you celebrate another day of life on this planet? How do you replenish yourself after expending energy and prepare yourself for the day ahead? Truth is, many of us don't really consider the start and end of the day. It just happens to us. We are rushed in the morning and exhausted at night. And then it starts all over again. As we look back at the day, we wonder why we didn't get as much done as we thought we would, or why we felt mildly irritated or dissatisfied. Maybe we were very busy but didn't actually accomplish anything.

Set your intentions and routines

Setting your intentions in the morning, and creating a routine or series of rituals, can make a dramatic difference in your day. You can manage your day rather than let it manage you. And at the end of the day, you can prepare yourself for another great day with a few evening rituals. You may be thinking that you are so busy that you can't possibly add any more to your day; however, by creating these morning and evening habits, you will find that you have more productive time in your days. This is because you move intentionally into the day rather than barreling into it and having your attention pulled in every direction.

When you set your intentions, you remind yourself of what is important so you can focus on that instead of every emerging crisis. You feel balanced and centered in the mind and the body, which helps maintain energy and focus during the day. You integrate and process the day's activities so you can learn from your experiences and take that into the next day. You rest well so you are more clear-headed the next day.

Rituals can make even the most mundane things a little more mindful. They give us a touchstone and, over time, the act of performing rituals can calm and restore us. And when we create our own rituals that help us cultivate mindfulness, we can move more intentionally into our days and nights.

Mindful mornings

So, back to those first moments of the day. Are you caught by surprise by the alarm clock? Are you rested or do you have to force yourself out of bed? Do you check the news or e-mails before you even get out of bed, starting the day with a feeling that you are already behind? What if you could change your perspective on the morning and change the whole day ahead?

The first hour is the rudder of the day. — Henry Ward Beecher

The first few moments of your day can really set the stage for the day ahead. It is a big transition to go from being fast asleep to actually getting up and moving around, yet some of us charge into the day without giving ourselves any time to make that change. To move mindfully in the morning, there are several areas of transition you have to go through— from being asleep to being awake, preparing the body to move, preparing the mind to think and focus, cleansing the body, nourishing the body, and preparing for the workday.

To really set up for the day, it is helpful to find a few rituals, or a morning routine, that is stable yet flexible. This is the rudder of your day and will set the course. When my alarm goes off, I do some gentle movement before getting out of bed. I exaggerate a yawn or two and stretch my entire body by either reaching my arms over my head, hugging my knees in to me, twisting a little, or circling my hands at my wrists and my feet at the ankles.

Once I get out of bed, I gaze at the sun so I can feel the transition from darkness to light, and mentally welcome the day ahead. As part of my morning routine, I brush my teeth and wash my face and then use the Neti pot—a nasal irrigation system that originally was part of the Ayurvedic tradition. (Now they are available everywhere, with easy instructions. You can use the Neti pot to rinse the sinus passages, allowing yourself to breathe more easily and clear out irritants. This can even help with allergies.) I also scrape my tongue—another gem from Ayurveda. Scraping the tongue helps clear off any buildup on the tongue, including bacteria. This also increases your taste reception, allowing you to feel more satisfied when you eat. And, psychologically, this brings an overall sense of clearing to the mind and the body.

Sometimes I'll body brush my skin to wake me up, exfoliate dead skin, and stimulate my lymphatic system. I'll also drink a glass of warm water to stimulate digestion and prepare my body for food. Then I move my body. This might be as simple as a walk around the block or a gentle Yoga practice. Or it might be an invigorating run or exercise class. Working out in the morning can really set the tone for a day of motivation and confidence.

I have to always eat a nourishing breakfast, as soon as I feel hungry. It helps stimulate my metabolism for the day. I drink decaf coffee, so I drink extra water, as coffee is a diuretic. I like to create a ritual around making and drinking it and to focus on my breakfast without multitasking. I feel fuller and more satisfied this way.

Once fed, I set my intention for the day. This may be as simple as articulating an intention to myself, or I may spend some time journaling and that may lead to my intention for the day. I write my to-do list and make sure it contains the activities that will not only get me through the day but will lead me to be satisfied at the end of the day.

Then I meditate. I simply sit for three or more minutes, becoming aware of my breath and my thoughts. This is a great check-in time for me to see what I might be carrying into the day. If I am feeling anxious, this is a great time to ask myself why that might be. This inquiry helps me move into the day with more clarity and keeps me more centered when things get crazy, as they most certainly will.

Finally, I make my commute mindful and make the most of it. I can be mindful, even in traffic. Red lights are my signal to take deep breaths. During long commutes I listen to a book or podcast that will educate and elevate me. And I give myself plenty of time to arrive; rushing and mindfulness do *not* go hand in hand. Depending on which of these I do, this can take between thirty minutes and two hours. My early wakeup gives me a lot of flexibility. Based on how you feel in the morning, you can create your own rituals.

Mindful evenings

Your transition into a mindful evening starts even before you leave work. Take some time to wrap up projects and organize your workspace for the next day, and decide that you will leave work at work. If you are not able to do that, decide what work you will do in the evening rather than allowing it to stretch out and take over your evening. And, again, make the most of your commute, using the time to create some space or separation between you and your workday.

Use your evening to renew and replenish for the next day. Make sure you have some activities that you really enjoy. If you enjoy cooking, making dinner can be a creative experience after work. If you don't like to cook, have easy-to-prepare foods available, or make plans to meet friends for dinner. Don't get surprised by dinner every night—have a plan that becomes your ritual.

Keep the mindfulness going at home. If you like to watch TV, that's fine, but create some boundaries. Only have the TV on when you are actually watching it, and don't binge until your eyes glaze over. Decide what you will watch, enjoy it, and then turn off the TV.

Put your phone away for a little while. Focus on whatever it is you are doing, whether talking to your family, eating dinner, listening to music, or straightening up the house.

Debrief the day. If you live with others, you can share highlights and lowlights from the day. Make it fun, and don't judge what the others say. If you live alone, you can do the same thing, perhaps writing it down or just reviewing it in your mind.

Turn off all screens an hour before you go to bed. This will help the body and mind relax. Instead of screen time, create a ritual around an evening walk or workout. If you do a strenuous workout, just be sure that it is not right before bed, as it may keep you from sleeping. Or gaze at the moon. Feel the nourishing energy of it and mentally welcome the night. Read a book or a magazine. Choose the material carefully; for some, reading disturbing or sad stories may keep you from falling asleep. Take a warm bath or shower.

Cultivate a gratitude practice. Take some time to review what you are grateful for. This can do wonders for helping you fall asleep as well. Meditate.

Take three or more minutes to sit quietly to watch the breath and your thoughts.

How to move forward with mindful routines

- ✓ Move out of bed gently.
- ✓ Create your own personal hygiene rituals.
- ✓ Move your body.
- ✓ Eat a good breakfast.
- ✓ Set your intention for the day. Meditate.
- ✓ Make your commutes mindful.
- ✓ Organize your workspace before you leave work to have it ready for the next day.
- ✓ Use your evening to wind down, debrief the day, and reenergize with a walk or warm bath.
- ✓ Turn of the media.
- ✓ Meditate.

These are just some ideas for making your mornings and evenings mindful. You may have other things that you do to help you head clearly into the day and wind down at the end of it. You don't need to do everything mentioned, but pick a few things that will help you create a morning and evening routine that sets you up for a successful day.

MINDFUL PRACTICE

Create your morning and evening rituals

1. Take a look at your mornings. What would you like to change? Are there things you are doing that are detracting from have a good morning? Select some rituals from the lists in the chapter and try them out. Give yourself extra time if you need, even considering waking up a little earlier so that you are not so rushed in the mornings. Think of other rituals that might be helpful to you. Perhaps it's something you have done in the past, or maybe something you have read about.
2. Take a look at your evenings. What would you like to change? Are there things you are doing that are keeping you from winding down in the evenings and getting a good night's sleep?

Mindful Nutrition

Nourish yourself in every way

*Remember that food is the most
basic link with the source of life. Be
thankful for it, pray over it, honor it.
We are not just filling our belly; we
are nurturing our mind and spirit as
well. Eating with full awareness puts
us in harmony with nature—not
only with the external world, but
also our own inner nature.*
— *Carrie Angus*

EATING. IT SHOULD BE AS SIMPLE AS
nourishing our bodies with the nutrients it needs. For

me, it has never really been simple. Food has always been about my weight, even from a young age. When I was young I was a gymnast. I was strong, with thighs like Mary Lou Retton; however, this was before Mary Lou Retton, so at the time, they were just big. My mother encouraged me to lose weight, so from my teenage years on, I fixated on that. In high school we all thought nothing of taking Dexatrim—a diet pill that was mostly caffeine. We did the banana diet and cabbage diet.

In college, I didn't quite gain the "freshman 15," but I did add a few pounds. Eventually I found my stride with regular exercise and pretty good nutrition. But I was still overly focused on food and what I could and couldn't eat; I was always trying to lose those last five pounds. Then came the Atkins diets, the Zone, paleo, veganism, low carbs, high carbs, good fats, and so much more. Sometimes I felt like there was nothing left that was okay to eat other than a cucumber or a carrot! But I knew there had to be more.

These days, I focus on being mindful about what I eat. I like what Michael Pollan wrote in *In Defense of Food:* "Eat food. Mostly plants. Not too much." I think that makes a lot of sense, but that is not all there is to this equation. It's not only what you eat, but how and why you eat that influences your body's nourishment. If I let myself get too freaked out about the latest food craze, then I am anxious when I eat and can't really enjoy my food. If I'm in a hurry, I eat too fast and don't even realize when I am full. If I eat on the run, I end up with some sort of digestive distress.

Why is healthy eating so hard?

First of all, we are busy, and stopping to prepare and eat food takes time. In the US, the average workweek is forty-nine hours, and 65 percent of workers eat lunch at their desks while working. Twenty percent of all meals are eaten in cars![1] Fast food seems more convenient, because when we are busy, nothing seems more convenient than driving through a line and having someone hand us a bag of food we can eat in the car. We always seem to be doing something else when we eat, so we don't pay attention to good nutrition. The CDC recommends 1 ½–2 cups of fruit and 2–3 cups of vegetables each day. Fresh foods, fruits, and vegetables take time to prepare, and only one in ten adults eats the recommended amount of fruit and vegetables.

On top of eating out of convenience and busyness, we carry a lot of associations and emotions around food that remind us of good times, relieve us of boredom, and comfort us. The good news is that as difficult as it is to develop new habits, if you keep it simple, you can make mindful changes.

> *By expanding the pleasure arising from the taste of eating and drinking, one should generate a mental state filled with that delight. As a result, supreme bliss will manifest. — Vijnana-Bhairava*

The current ADA guidelines are simple and flexible: Follow a healthy eating pattern; focus on variety, nutrient density, and amount; limit calories from added sugars and saturated fats; reduce sodium intake; shift to healthier food and beverage choices; and support healthy eating patterns for all. I like this because it focuses on improvement, not perfection. Even small changes can make a difference. As you get started, there's no point in biting off more than you can chew (pun intended).

Simple guidelines to move to more mindful eating

Once you've made a decision to change a habit, there are many ways to signal to yourself that you are committed. You need to create some kind of discontinuity so that you don't fall back into old habits. You could read a book about it (as you are right now), join a class or support group, or find an accountability buddy. Some people are self-motivated and others need someone to help them. Do what works best for you.

1. First, take an honest look at your current eating habits

Food logs are helpful when looking to create change. To be mindful, you need to look not only at *what* you are eating, but *how, why,* and *when* you are eating. You can use one of the many apps out there, or you can just keep notes in a journal. On a daily basis, record what you eat, when you eat, and how hungry you are when you eat. Don't get too caught up in calories or quantities, just do your best descriptions—this will be the benchmark from which you will make improvements. Noting *when* you eat will help you assess how your distribution of food over the course of the day affects how you feel, your energy levels, and whether or not you head to the fridge right before bed. By paying attention to how hungry you are when you eat, you can begin to see when you are eating because you are hungry, or if you are eating for other reasons—triggers that cause you to eat when you are not actually hungry, or just the fact that it's a mealtime and others are eating. Journaling how you eat is also worth noting—do you sit down calmly and eat slowly or stand up? Do you eat while watching TV or looking at your phone? Exercise you do in the day and the amount of water you drink can also affect your eating habits, so note that too.

Do this for two weeks, including weekends, and you will begin to see patterns. Then you can decide which patterns you want to address.

2. Do your best and be kind to yourself

Don't berate yourself for your current habits, and don't expect results overnight. Acknowledge your efforts to make a healthy, mindful change, and use the information as data points for moving forward. Aim for better choices, not perfection. If you try to eat perfectly, you will likely get disappointed and discouraged. Celebrate the small changes.

3. All foods fit

If your diet is too restricted, you may feel deprived and resentful. Eat the foods you like and allow yourself to enjoy every bite.

4. Prepare your food with intention

It does take some time to pull a meal together, but you can save time by buying precut or pre-prepped food if you are strapped for time. However, if you can dedicate just a little bit of time to food preparation, this will increase the mindfulness of the whole process. You can prep the food when you have some extra time. Set aside an hour or two on the weekend to prep food for the week. When it is time to make your meal, set an intention about nourishing yourself and enjoy the creative process.

5. When you eat, only eat

Turn off the TV and put down your phone. Step away from your computer. If you are with others, then certainly you will talk and interact, but don't let that get in the way of really noticing what you are eating. Look at your food and notice the colors and shapes on your plate. Take in the smells. When you finally taste your food, really pay attention to the flavors and textures.

6. Eat slowly

We tend to rush through everything, and that includes eating. If you really pay attention, it is actually difficult to eat quickly. Even if no one else around you is eating slowly, take time to chew your food thoroughly and finish one bit before you start the next one. Drink any liquids slowly too. You will be amazed that you will feel fuller with less food, and you will digest your food more easily.

7. Fuel yourself throughout the day

Breakfast plans

As soon as you are hungry, eat breakfast. A healthy breakfast feeds the brain and wakes up your digestive system. You prime the metabolism and get some fuel to start the day. Breakfast doesn't have to be complicated, just balanced. My go-to breakfast rotation is eggs scrambled with veggies; oatmeal with nuts and fruit; whole grain toast with almond butter or avocado; and smoothie with protein, fruits, and veggies.

Snack plans

Keep yourself from getting too hungry during the day. While I have found it suits me best to eat three good meals with no snacks, that doesn't work for everyone. If you do snack, make sure you always have healthy snacks available, because if you don't, you might only find high-sugar and high-fat options within reach. Try to combine protein, carbohydrates, and fats in a snack, and only snack in small portions when you are hungry. Don't snack right before mealtimes either. While it's tempting to use coffee to curb your appetite, your body is telling you it needs some nutrition. Plan ahead if you know your body will need extra food on any given day, keeping in consideration your activity level. It's helpful to snack on something healthy, too, if you're hungry, before going to an office birthday or other celebrations.

Some of my snack choices

Fruit with peanut butter or almonds
Nuts and dried fruit
Smoothie
Veggies and hummus
Popcorn

Lunch plans

For lunch, be sure to plan ahead. You can bring a healthy lunch to work and step away from your desk for a midday break. If the weather is nice, you can eat outside. If you are going out for lunch, you might have a midmorning snack so you are not too hungry. If you can, check out the menu or options and have a plan before you go so that you can make nourishing choices. Below is a list of mindful options for when you're having lunch out.

Mindful food options	
Do	**Don't**
Choose steamed, poached, baked, or stir-fried items	Eat everything on your plate just because it's there
Choose broiled, baked, and grilled options for meat, chicken, and fish	Choose crispy, creamy, cheesy, breaded, battered, or fried food
Eat your vegetables	Be afraid of asking for what you want
Ask for sauce and dressing on the side	Get empty calories from soft drinks or juices
Take home extra or too much food	Get your very own dessert

If you eat a reasonably portioned, balanced lunch, your body will thank you, and you may find that you don't have an energy slump in the afternoon. If you have overeaten, or eaten, a very heavy lunch, your body will take what it needs and then have to figure out what to do with the rest. This can stress your system. On the other hand, if you don't eat enough, you may find your energy waning as well. Over time, with mindful eating, you will intuitively know how to eat to manage your energy in the afternoons. If you do need afternoon snacks, apply the same principles from the morning snack, and don't go home too hungry.

Dinner plans

To be sure you continue your mindfulness into the evening meal, do some advance planning. For years I was "surprised" by dinner every single night and had a flash of panic when it was time to prepare the final meal of the day. Dinner happens just about every night, and with some organization, it can be a lovely way to end the workday and transition into the evening.

I've found that planning for dinner before preparation time can be a game changer. I do some planning, shopping, and prepping over the weekend, or anytime I have a little time, and it's been a huge turning point. I also splurged and bought the right kitchen tools—some really good knives, a slow cooker, and a food processor to make prep faster and so much more enjoyable.

I also learned a few time-saving techniques. When I ate meat, poaching chicken breasts and freezing them made mealtime really simple. I poached them over the weekend; shredded some for use in enchiladas, soups, or salads; and threw them in the freezer. Sometimes I will bake potatoes in advance, as well, and prepare rice and pasta. Anything that can be done in advance helps.

Traveling plans

It's always harder to eat mindfully when we're on the road, but there are a few things I try to do that help. The main thing is that I'll stop the car to get out and look for a place to sit down and eat. That way I can take a break, stretch, and focus on enjoying what I'm eating. I also plan for regular snacks and meals by looking at the day ahead to see when I can schedule those times in. I stock up on "whole" food bars or snacks and don't let myself get too hungry, and if I haven't prepared anything and must eat fast food, I eat small portions.

We often confuse thirst for hunger when we just need to drink more, and it's important to stay hydrated. Drink water at room/car temperature and avoid sugary or diet drinks.

Stock your pantry

Incorporate meal planning into your overall planning for the week—stock your pantry with convenient, healthy staples so you don't have to run to the store at the last minute. Here are a few ideas to get you started:

- Quick cooking oats
- Coconut oil

- Honey
- Quinoa
- Olive oil
- Decaf or herbal tea
- Nuts
- Vinegars
- Almond milk
- Sesame oil
- Brown rice
- Frozen vegetables and fruit
- Sugar-free protein powder
- Tamari or Bragg Liquid Aminos
- Onions
- Garlic
- Cumin, cinnamon, ginger

Always look for healthier options. Some interesting swaps are:

— Mashed cauliflower instead of mashed potatoes

— Corn tortillas instead of tortilla chips

— Tea with mint or fruit, sparkling water with flavored vinegar instead of soft drinks

— Dark chocolate instead of milk chocolate

— Oven-baked fries or chickpeas instead of french fries

— Plain yogurt with fruit instead of sweetened
yogurt

— Homemade pasta or vegetable spirals instead of
conventional pasta

How to move forward with mindful nutrition

✓ Keep a food log for two weeks, then review
your habits and choose one or two issues to
address every two or three weeks.

✓ Eat each meal sitting down and focus on the
company and the food.

✓ Plan ahead for daily snacks and travel.

✓ Eat food that will bless your body.

✓ Stay hydrated by drinking plenty of water
throughout the day.

MINDFUL PRACTICE

1. What are your food triggers?
   — What creates a need to eat when you are not hungry?
   — How can you address that?
   — How can you bring more balance into your eating?
2. Experiment in the kitchen with a new recipe each week. Create a cookbook of your favorites.

*For recipes, and much more, visit my website: www.beingwellyoga/recipes. I've also put some of my favorite recipes in the back of this book to get you started.

Mindful Meditation Practices

Get quiet so you can listen to yourself

In the midst of movement and chaos, keep stillness inside of you. — Deepak Chopra

IF YOU TALK TO ANYONE about meditation, you will find that the word conjures up all kinds of thoughts and feelings. For many, it is a scary concept. For others, it has a religious connotation. It is something a lot of people wish they did but don't know how to start, and many talk about how it has changed their lives.

For our purposes, I will define meditation, outline why it is beneficial, and suggest some different techniques for doing it. I'll keep it very simple, because it really is. Yet, like so many things that are simple, we humans can easily complicate them! I'll also talk about some common pitfalls and how to avoid them.

What is meditation?

Meditation is practicing mindfulness while being seated or choosing some other still or stable position. It can be thought of as contemplation or reflection. It is a technique to give our usually busy minds a mini-vacation from the jobs of thinking, organizing, managing, directing, and trying to control the world around us. It is the opposite of doing—it is just being.

And that is very hard for many of us who are conditioned to a life of doing. As you saw in month 5, we have so many ways to fill our time with inputs that the mind doesn't get to take many breaks during our waking hours. It can be uncomfortable to look into the mind and peel off the layers of thoughts, beliefs, emotions, and other perceptions and just *be* with our true selves. For those unaccustomed to any quiet at all, it can take a while before the noise of the mind subsides enough to get a glimpse of the true self. However, when it happens, it can be a revelation, a relief, and a gift.

I work for myself and have a flexible schedule, but I still have to intentionally set aside time to renew during the day, otherwise I find myself really depleted at the end of the day. I am a fairly energetic person, and often, when I have a lot to do, I find myself getting worn out, yet I keep going. On any given day, I may teach a couple of classes, do some writing and planning, have a private session, follow up with corporate clients or retreat plans, or catch up on administrative work. It's nothing crazy, but it really seems like there is always more to do than I have time for. Even when it seems like I won't get everything done, it always helps me to take a 15–30-minute meditation break. Sometimes I will listen to a recorded guided meditation; sometimes I will sit quietly and watch my breath; sometimes I will chant a mantra. It doesn't really matter which technique I use; I always feel better afterwards and ready to get back to work.

It's really good for you

There have been over 19,000 studies done on the effects of meditation. The benefits of 5–10 minutes of quiet meditation each day range from increased feelings of well-being to changes in the brain that can improve memory and decrease fear. Here are some of the biggies when it comes to the benefits of meditation:

Stress reduction
When we sit quietly and take a look at our thoughts, we can separate from them and regain perspective. When we have this perspective, our stressful thoughts lose some of their control over us and we feel more empowered, which lets us deal with stressful situations with more confidence and calmness, rather than getting more and more wrapped up in the stress.

Less anxiety, fear, and depression
Just as with the above, when looking at ourselves free of the moment-to-moment agitation in the mind that often accompanies us through the day, we can regain some perspective. We can look at our worries and fears from a short distance rather than completely identify with them. We give ourselves a break, which

often relieves us of the intensity of our thoughts and emotions.

> The ordinary mind, being a machine, has but one function: it creates and then goes about attempting to solve problems! It enjoys this game and will continue to play it as long as you allow it to do so, throughout your entire life if it can. It is not concerned that you are suffering in many areas because of its games. You will come to understand through meditation techniques that *you are not your ordinary mind* and that it has not nearly the importance which we attach to it.

— Richard Hittleman, *Guide to Yoga Meditation*

Improved concentration
We've gotten very good at being fragmented. Practicing being still and simply noticing what is happening in the moment can help us regain the ability to focus and concentrate.

Increased self-awareness
This seems obvious, because we are sitting still and being with ourselves. This self-awareness can be helpful and empowering as we navigate relationships, jobs, and all of our endeavors. With self-awareness,

we can begin to recognize and change destructive or unhelpful habits.

Improved health

By inducing relaxation, meditation causes blood vessels to open up and decreases blood pressure levels. It improves heart rate, breathing, and brain waves. Meditation also improves immunity.

Now that you have an idea of just some of the benefits of meditation, let's get started.

Cultivating a meditation practice

To begin a meditation practice, first you must release your preconceived notions and any desire for control. Come into the practice without expectation. There is no such thing as good or bad meditation. There is no way to do it wrong, so take the pressure off yourself. Just resolve to be mindful with it and see what happens each time you meditate.

Have patience and trust the process. As I tell my students, when you sit down, get quiet, and take a good look at what is going on, it's definitely not all rainbows and unicorns! There are lots of reasons we don't get quiet that often, the main one being it can be really hard to look at what is truly going on. And when we begin, we may just need to deal with a lot of noise and old conditioning in the brain before we can look at our true selves. Take all of these things as messengers or data points. It is really good to see what your mind is habitually turning to. In my meditations, I often find myself rehashing whatever TV show I recently watched—perhaps a data point to tell me that I am watching a bit too much television, or using it as a way to escape from what is really happening with me! There is no perfection here, just a process of tuning in and noticing what *is*. There are also no goals. You may set an intention to be mindful or alert for a certain amount of time, but please don't set goals for your meditation practice. If you do, you put yourself out of *being* and back into *doing*. We already do enough of that!

Sometimes it is beyond challenging to sit quietly, and sometimes the time passes in the blink of an eye. Sometimes you feel grounded and strong, and sometimes your back hurts and your nose itches and you think your meditation timer surely must be broken. Simply release judgment, accept whatever happens, and have compassion for yourself.

Start small. In the beginning, it may be challenging to sit even for five minutes, so start with one minute. Any amount of time is fine, as long as you are designating that time and space for a meditation practice. Over time, you will be able to sit for longer periods. If sitting on the floor is not comfortable, sit in a chair. I've found that if you go out and tell all your friends about your new awesome meditation practice, it puts expectations on you and takes your focus away. If you need accountability, try scheduling your meditation time on your calendar, or use an app like Insight Timer that helps you track your meditation sessions.

I'm ready. . . . Now what?

There are many ways to meditate. Here we will explore just a few simple ways.

1. Breath meditation

In this meditation, the breath becomes the object of your attention. You simply watch or notice the breath as it comes in, and watch or notice the breath as it goes out. You don't try to change or manage the breath; you just observe. When the mind wanders away from the breath, just come back to it as soon as you notice that the mind has wandered. The practice brings the awareness back to the breath time and time again.

2. Sitting with yourself and your thoughts

In this meditation, the thoughts become the objects of your awareness. You watch your thoughts as they surface, but you don't attach to, or get involved with, your thoughts. You just watch. As you watch, feelings and emotions will arise as well, and you watch those too. Try not to judge your thoughts, push them away, or change them. When you notice a thought, your reaction can just be a noncommittal *hmm* to acknowledge the thought, and then you can let it go and let the next one come. With regular practice, the mind will eventually settle down and release the thoughts on its own. You may have glimpses of yourself beneath all of the thoughts, and you can just *be* with the stillness and experience that.

3. Mantra meditation

Mantra means "instrument of the mind." If you use a mantra during your meditation, the mantra gives the mind something to do while you sit, and that "something" is not attached to your thinking. It can be helpful if you are in monkey mind mode with the mind jumping from thought to thought. You can say the mantra silently to yourself, or you can say it out loud. There are many mantras you can find on various meditation apps to accompany you, if that is helpful.

The mantra can be anything at all. It can be in English or any other language. A very helpful and simple mantra is to say to yourself on the inhale *Let* and say to yourself on the exhale *Go.*

4. Guided meditation

Having someone else guide you through a meditation can be a good way to get started as well. There are many apps that have guided meditations of varying lengths. I practice a guided meditation called *Yoga Nidra,* which means conscious sleep. This allows the thinking mind to relax while the body is still awake (well, usually, that is!). A guided meditation can be particularly helpful for those who have experienced trauma and have more challenges just getting quiet with themselves.

How to move forward with mindful meditation practices

✓ Intentionally set aside time to renew during the day.

✓ Choose a quiet, soothing place to meditate in.

✓ Start small and remember there are no goals.
✓ Choose any technique you would like each day.
✓ Be flexible and open to your practice as it
  evolves and grows!

As with many things in this book, this is just the tip of the iceberg, and you can continue your studies in meditation as you begin to explore this mindful practice. Enjoy the purity of simply being and watch how this begins to shift your perspective when you are out in the world.

MINDFUL PRACTICE

1. Which time of the day seems to work best for your meditation practice? Maybe it's the first thing or the last thing you do each day. Maybe it's a break in the middle of a busy day.
2. Where would be a good, quiet, uncluttered place to practice in—one where you feel comfortable and won't be disturbed?
3. Find a meditation app or timer to set for your meditation so that you won't be tempted to look at your watch or a clock during your session. Start with three minutes and adjust from there.
4. When your meditation session is over, take a few moments with whatever feelings are now present. Journal about your experience.

*For recordings of the meditations in this chapter, and much more, visit my website: www.beingwellyoga.com/nidrapractice

Mindful Communication

Bring out your authentic voice

Wise men speak because they have something to say. Fools speak because they have to say something. — Plato

WHEN WAS THE LAST TIME you really paid attention to what someone was saying? When was the last time you felt that someone was really listening to you? Do you ever meet someone and immediately forget his or her name? Are you ever caught off guard when asked a question during a meeting because you were not paying attention?

If we are honest with ourselves, when we are interacting with others, we are often not giving them our full, undivided attention. And because of that, communication suffers and relationships often pay the price. This leads to misunderstandings, hurt feelings, mistakes, and regrets.

Even when we think we are being mindful, our habits can keep us from communicating authentically; that is, we are not truly sharing or interacting in a way that is true to ourselves. This can cause us to feel anxious and depressed, and can keep us from connecting with others.

Communication that is not mindful also leads to mistakes and inefficiencies. At work, this can impede productivity and quickly demotivate, and even demoralize a team. It doesn't have to be that way.

We can bring our mindful practices to communication. We can bring awareness and openness to our interactions and relationships rather than just bringing our old habits, practices, and stories to our conversations.

For me the challenge is letting go of needing to complete tasks and really stopping to listen. When my daughter is home from college, I am so excited to catch up with her. However, I do find myself continuing to work even when she is talking to me, and of course she notices. So many times she asks me if I heard what she just said and I have to honestly admit that I haven't. Multitasking simply does not go with good communication. So now I consciously stop what I am doing to put my full attention on the person I am with. That means putting down my phone, not typing e-mails while talking on the phone, and looking right at the person I am with. It's even more challenging on the phone when I don't have the person to look at, but it can be done. Focus mindfully on the interaction and watch communication improve.

The obstacles

There are a lot of reasons why we don't always communicate mindfully. When a person comes to talk to us, we may already have a preconceived notion of what that person will say, how he or she will say it, and what the person wants. When this happens, we hear what we think we are going to hear rather than actually listen to what is being said.

At other times, we are too busy or distracted to listen and we see talking as an interruption. Instead of letting a person know there may be a better time to talk, we don't really listen because we are thinking about or doing something else. And then when we do attempt to listen, we are thinking about our response rather than what is being said. This happens all the time! We are so focused about what we need to say that we stop listening for understanding and just wait for a time when we can reply.

We often don't speak our truth. We fear that if we do, the other person or people will not like us, or that we may become unpopular. It sounds very "high school," but it continues long after that period of life, especially if we feel a bit unsure of ourselves. We don't really know how to express our feelings. Depending on how we were raised, our work experiences, or really any experiences, we may have learned that we have to keep our true feelings bottled up rather than express them. This can lead to more missed connection.

Perhaps, most importantly, we forget that communication involves talking *and* listening. It involves connecting rather than commanding. It is about sharing and collaborating, not dictating what we want. We also forget that how we communicate with ourselves is as important, and often the key, to how we communicate with others.

> *We have two ears and one mouth so we can listen twice*
> *as much as we speak. — Epictetus*

How do you talk to yourself?

Most of us don't walk around talking to ourselves out loud, but we do carry an inner dialogue. This often involves dredging up our past mistakes or projecting to the uncertain future. We berate ourselves for making a mistake, bringing up all of the times we did stupid things. We feel anxious, and, rather than giving ourselves a pep talk, we remind ourselves of what losers we are.

If you think about it, do you talk to yourself the way that you would talk to your most loyal lifelong friend? Why not? Who have you known longer? Who has been with you through more experiences? You really are your most loyal, constant lifelong companion, so why not treat yourself like your very best friend? If you begin to talk to yourself with more caring and compassion, you will find that your inner dialogue becomes more mindful and much more helpful. You will likely find that it soon becomes easier to talk mindfully to others when you are comfortable communicating with awareness to yourself.

Listening is a skill that can be honed

How good a listener are you? Do you give your full attention to the person who is speaking?

When someone talks to you, try putting down your phone and not looking at it. If your phone notifies you every time you get an e-mail or text, you can turn off the alerts, or have some designated times of the day when your phone is set to Do Not Disturb. You may miss the distractions at first, but you will be giving the speaker your full attention. You both may be surprised at how much more satisfying the interaction is.

The mind can jump around like a crazed monkey. It's up to you whether or not you allow that. You may often identify with your thoughts so much that you think they are who you are. With your meditation practices, or even simple awareness, you can begin to separate and observe your thoughts rather than continuously be connected to them. By doing something to disconnect from them, you can signal to your thoughts that it is time for them to take a break. This can be as simple as changing your body position and looking directly at the person talking. You may want to take a walk with the person, or change the environment, to signal to yourself that it's time to listen.

We have too many judges in our minds. When someone is talking, we may have already decided what the person is going to say, and whether he or she is right or wrong. Each time your feel a judgment coming up, notice it and mindfully set it aside so that you can again listen. Ask questions to be sure you have understood without bias.

We also have a habit of formulating what we are going to say, while the person is talking, when we could commit to listening instead. Really focus on understanding and hearing what the person is saying. After the person finishes, take a deep breath and consider what you really want to say. Then, and only then, begin talking. This takes a lot of patience and practice.

All of your mindfulness practices are leading you to be able to listen better—first to yourself and then to others. When you watch your mind and detach from it, that is great practice for listening to someone else and detaching from that as well.

Clarity

Speaking clearly, and in a focused way, starts with your intention. I already mentioned that your intention is *how* you want to move into something, not just *what* you will do. For communication, it's the same—*how* you communicate sets the stage for *what* you communicate. This, in itself, can help lead to more clarity in your communication. When you let your intention to communicate with clarity lead you, you will be less likely to get jumbled up in multiple agendas and ideas. You will be less impatient and will spend the time solely on communicating well.

Before you speak, consider your intention for speaking. Why are you saying what you are saying? While this may be cumbersome in daily conversations, over time this consideration can become a habit. For more formal speaking, such as presentations, this consideration is crucial. I worked for a boss who would review a presentation and say, "Where are you leading me?" Each point had to be consistent and intentionally lead to the next so that the conclusion, or close, would be inevitably clear.

Authenticity

We want to speak and listen from our hearts, but often the ego or our insecurity gets in the way, and we say what we think we should rather than what we feel.

As you move through the year, incorporating mindfulness along the way, your authentic voice will get stronger and stronger until it is no longer practical to keep it under wraps. As you communicate with others, be sure that you first communicate with yourself to understand what is important to you. Then you will be able to bring your authentic voice out. As Don Miguel Ruiz writes in his book *The Four Agreements,* "Always be impeccable with your word—bringing your truth out is the right use of your energy."

Kindness and compassion

When we become mindful, we realize that we truly are all connected. If we can speak kindly and compassionately to ourselves, we will be able to do the same with others. We can ask ourselves if what we are saying is true, kind, and necessary. This will keep us from blurting out something hurtful to another when we are feeling bad about ourselves. Get in the habit of speaking in this way and you will be amazed at the kindness and compassion that comes back to you.

Yogi Bhajan, the yogi who introduced Kundalini Yoga to the US, had some timeless rules for communication, which I've placed at the end of this chapter. I love studying and practicing Kundalini because it focuses on moving energy, which is great for removing communication blocks. Some of these rules resonate more than others for me. I hope you find something there that speaks to you.

How to move forward with mindful communication

✓ Become aware of how you speak to yourself. Look for patterns. Begin to practice self-talk that is kind and compassionate. Be sure to congratulate yourself appropriately when you do.

✓ Do you fall into certain judgments or assumptions with some people? Do you interrupt? Practice mindful listening with your full attention.

✓ Try mindful listening with someone with whom you have a difficult relationship and see what changes.

✓ The throat is the energy center, or chakra, responsible for communication. Notice how the throat feels when communication is easeful and how it feels when communication is difficult. Notice how the throat feels when you are speaking authentically versus saying something to be accepted or to avoid conflict. This can be a great signal for when change is needed.

MINDFUL PRACTICE

1. Keep a listening journal. At the end of the day, write down the discussions you had. Note the following:
   — Subject of discussion
   — Who talked more—you or the other person?
   — What do you know now?
   — Were you able to listen fully before answering?
   — Did you ask questions to lead to greater understanding?
   — Did you listen while looking at your phone?
   — Did you listen while thinking about something else?
   — Did you listen while waiting for the first opportunity to jump in with your awesome comeback?
   — Did you listen while assuming the other person was wrong?
   — Did you listen without valuing the other person?
2. Take notes for several discussions a week and look for trends. Journal your learning and improvements.

Harmonious Communication

You are communicating for a better tomorrow, not to spoil today.

Whatever you are going to say is going to live forever. And you have to live through it. Therefore, take care that you don't have to live through the mud of your own communication.

One wrong word can do much more wrong than you can ever imagine or even estimate.

Words spoken are a chance for communication. Don't turn them into a war.

When you communicate, you have to communicate again. Don't make the road rough.

— from a lecture by Yogi Bhajan

Mindful Conflict Resolution

Resolve issues with compassion and understanding

Out beyond ideas of wrongdoing and rightdoing there is a field. I will meet you there. — Rumi

IT SEEMS LIKE A GOOD TIME to talk about something we love to avoid—conflict. Conflict is inevitable—it will never go away and it is often unresolved. But we all tend to dream of a life free of conflict. This chapter is about mindfully managing your inner and outer reactions to conflict. This will also help you move toward more collaboration rather than competition.

A life free of conflict? Think about how boring that would be! Different ideas, opinions, perspectives, beliefs, ways of working, and even ways of living make life rich, full, and interesting. A passionate exchange of different ideas can lead to creative and game-changing outcomes. Heated debates help us to clarify what is important to us and see what may be important to others. Yet most people dread or avoid conflict. What can we do to actually befriend conflict and embrace all that it has to offer?

I actually have learned to love conflict. I find it releases a lot of tension and clears the air. I used to sit with an issue and really stew over it, but I don't do that anymore. I'll give you an example: I teach Yoga at several studios, and I am my own best advocate when it comes to asking to be paid what I think I am worth. Recently I asked for an increase at a studio and was turned down. The reasons were solid and had more to do with the business than with me, and I accepted that. A few months later, I learned that other teachers had received increases; and, of course, I felt I deserved mine. Rather than create stories in my mind about it, get my feelings hurt, or dash off a passive-aggressive e-mail, I had a discussion with the studio owner. I shared what I had learned and gave my reasons for an increase. We had an open and honest discussion about all of the contributing factors and based on our shared understanding of value and the work done, I received my increase. It could have gone the other way as well. What was important was that I initiated an open and honest discussion and we came to an agreement, even though we started out in different places.

What is conflict?

A common understanding is that conflict is the friction or opposition resulting from actual or perceived differences or incompatibilities. Many of the words in this definition sound negative, but we know that conflict is not always negative, although we perceive it to be. Another definition is that conflict is the juxtaposition of different ideas, beliefs, and values. That sounds pretty good; however, by definition, conflict is the discord that happens when these differing opinions, ideas, etc. are present.

If we are mindful, though, discord is not negative either; it's another opportunity for self-inquiry, which leads to self-understanding.

Inner conflicts and external conflicts

Inner conflicts

- Are based on conditioning and beliefs
- Are created in the mind and felt in the body
- Cause us to "fight" with ourselves—we resist, push away, avoid, or obsess
- Make us feel alone or stuck

External conflicts

- Come from people, roles, situations, environment
- Stem from wanting to control situations or outcomes, *or* our feelings and projections
- Are based on our interaction with the world and habits in dealing with it
- Hold a shared responsibility to resolve the conflict (or we alone cannot resolve the conflict)
- Cause us to move into fight or flight mode

Mindfulness practices can help with both internal and external conflict and judgments.

Mindful Conflict Management	
Inner	**External**
Mindfulness helps us shift our perspective to acceptance.	We acknowledge our participation and responsibility rather than feeling like the victim (this is happening "to me").
We become a participatory observer rather than a judge.	We observe our reactions.
We cultivate compassion.	We prepare to listen rather than react.
We can see more clearly into the nature of our stories	We cultivate flexibility.
We can dis-identify with our stories so that they lose their power.	We look for common ground and connection.
We accept our identity.	We let go of a winners' and losers' mentality.

When dealing with conflict, two statements really help me. First is a seemingly paradoxical statement.

"The opposite of what you believe is also true."
— Zen Buddhist Koan

and another from Yogi Bhajan, which is,

"Recognize that the other person is you."
— Yogi Bhajan

Everything exists on a continuum, yet we are trained to think of the opposition at the ends of the continuum. In dealing with conflict, it is helpful to practice mindfulness that allows you to hold opposites at the same time. There is more to every story than just what you think. The mind has a hard time recognizing opposites, but the body is able to feel its way into this.

Next time you are about to step into a conflict (or feel the urge to run away from a conflict), take your mindfulness pause. Rather than focusing on the fight, focus on staying relaxed and open. Notice when you are provoked and what provokes you and breathe and relax into that. Take that information into a self-inquiry session later—sitting quietly or journaling to understand what triggers you.

When I talked about communication in month 9, I said that to truly listen, we have to let go of our preconceived notions and judgments. This is even more important when seeking to resolve conflict. Be open and listen. This is probably not about you or the other person, but about solving a problem, so let go of your story and listen to his or hers.

Observe what is happening. Feel the tension and the resistance in your body and breath. Breathe and open into that rather than allow it to escalate or close you down. Continue to breathe long, deep breaths to keep yourself from getting winded or agitated. The breath also allows you to remain present rather than dig up the past or project out to the future.

You don't have to win the discussion. Conflict can be resolved, or at least explored, with both parties remaining whole. We all lose when we believe it has to be either/or. This understanding can expand our awareness and our possibilities.

Conflict meditation

Become aware of something that is creating stress or conflict for you. Feel the reactions in the mind and the body. Stay with these in a nonjudgmental fashion and notice what arises. Don't try to fix anything; just be with what is.

You can become much more comfortable and adept at dealing with conflict. A lot of the practice for this happens before the actual conflict. Meditating on opposites is particularly helpful. I use and teach iRest Yoga Nidra for this.[1]

When meditating on opposites, we look at various aspects such as a sensation in the body, or a belief or emotion that is present. We feel where it is in the body and then call upon its opposite and ask ourselves to feel that. We alternate between one and the other, and eventually we hold both at the same time in our bodies. It is a great way to let go of that either/or thinking.

It's not always easy, and it takes a lot of practice, but it will get easier with time. Move into conflict with compassion for yourself and others, and you will find that the richness of new perspectives can expand your horizons in wonderful new ways.

How to move forward with mindful conflict resolution

- ✓ Rather than avoid conflict, take your mindfulness pause and then address the situation.
- ✓ Stay present.
- ✓ Let go of your story.
- ✓ Focus on your body.
- ✓ Focus on your breath.
- ✓ Remember you don't have to win the discussion every time.
- ✓ Notice when you are creating either/or thinking and find a new way to look at the situation that is not polarizing.

MINDFUL PRACTICE

1. Over the course of this month, notice the following about your conflicts:
   — Describe the situation.
   — How did it come about?
   — What did you really want?
   — What did the other person really want?
   — How did you feel?
   — How did you act?
   — How was the situation resolved?
   — If the situation wasn't resolved, how can it be resolved?

2. Record the answers to these questions in your journal.

Mindful Gratitude

Give thanks and enjoy the bounty in your life

When I started counting my blessings, my whole life turned around. — Willie Nelson

THANK YOU. IT'S A SIMPLE PHRASE, and one we hear and say often; however, about half the time it is just said out of habit. People don't send thank-you notes, or rarely even acknowledge a gift of kindness, anymore. Perhaps things have become casual, or perhaps we take things for granted more than we used to.

One of my pet peeves is going in to buy something and not being thanked for my purchase. Sometimes I wait for it, and if nothing is said, I just head out. Sometimes I will say thank you when my purchase is handed to me, expecting to hear thank you in return. Instead I usually hear, "No problem." I take a deep breath and resist the urge to sarcastically say, Really? It's no problem for you to take my money and have me support your business?

That's a bit of a silly example. My point is that giving thanks is important. It feels good to the person who gives thanks and to the person who receives thanks, and it's part of mindful living, because we pay attention to the goodness in our lives and allow ourselves to feel grateful for it. A 2016 study done by the Merci Chocolate Company found that Americans say thank you 2,000 times a year; that's about 5.5 times a day. Giving thanks, however, is just the tip of the iceberg in developing mindful gratitude practices.

> Years ago I had a Buddhist teacher in Thailand who would remind all his students that there was always something to be thankful for. He'd say, "Let's rise and be thankful, for if we didn't learn a lot today, at least we may have learned a little. And if we didn't learn even a little, at least we didn't get sick.

And if we did get sick, at least we didn't die. So let us all be thankful."

— Leo Buscaglia, *Born for Love: Reflections on Loving*

What is mindful gratitude?

Mindful gratitude is about having an appreciation for all that life has to offer. It's beyond just being thankful when you get what you want or when things go your way. It's being grateful for the experience of being alive. It's finding the good or helpful in our challenges, as well as our victories. We have not necessarily been taught to be grateful for the things we don't get, or the things that disappoint us. Mindful practice helps us to regain perspective and let go of our expectations and conditioned responses so that we can fully experience and live each moment—a worthy pursuit.

I already say thank you 5.5 times a day. What's so great about a gratitude practice?

There have been numerous studies done on the benefits of gratitude. Gratitude can improve everything—from helping you sleep better, to having more friends, to improving brain function, to living longer. There are no studies that claim that gratitude practices are not worthwhile, or even neutral about the benefits. They are really, really effective. Here are a few more benefits, from the expected to the more surprising:

- Better relationships
- Less physical pain
- Career success
- Happier
- Less self-centered
- Increased resiliency
- Improved self-esteem
- Greater likeliness to exercise
- Stronger marriages
- Reduced toxic emotions

> *It's not happy people who are thankful. It's thankful people who are happy. — Stamped on a coffee mug*

How do we cultivate gratitude?

Setting an intention to be grateful put me on the path to paying attention to the abundance in my life, and I began to recognize and enjoy life's simple pleasures. I changed my perspective. Even when things are not going my way now, I look for things to be thankful for in the midst of disappointments. I also focus on appreciating and acknowledging nice things others do for me, or something that helps me. I'm a big fan of thank-you notes and send them out of appreciation. It makes me feel great, and the recipients feel great too.

When I sit down to a meal, I appreciate all that went into bringing that nourishing meal to the table—mother nature and the farmers, factory workers, distributors, people who thought of and produced the appliances and utensils I am using, and the ones who prepared the food. It can help me feel connected, mindful, and awestruck even to sit down to enjoy a bowl of soup!

I appreciate my body, especially my legs and feet, for carrying me on my walk and moving me forward. I feel grateful for a gentle breeze or the warmth of the sun on my skin. I appreciate the park service and the individuals who built the path I am walking on. I thank the trees for their beauty, strength, and fruit.

When I have a long commute ahead and I don't like it too much, I focus on gratitude for the roads that carry me, and for the introduction of automobiles or trains or planes. I have a favorite radio station and I am grateful that it plays my favorite songs. I am also grateful for podcasts, NPR, and hands-free technology so I can catch up with friends while the miles roll by.

When I go to work, I allow myself to feel grateful for the ability to contribute to something greater than myself; for my thinking mind; for collaboration, or even for conflict, that might allow new ideas to surface. I'm grateful that my work allows me to purchase things I need to live.

It is also important to be able to receive gratitude. We are often hesitant to receive compliments or thanks, and we might even brush them off. Allow yourself to receive as well as give; it's a lovely way to bring balance to your gratitude practice.

We have so much to be thankful for. Challenge yourself to bring gratitude into your daily activities and watch the shift happen.

Begin and end the day with gratitude

As I mentioned in month 6, rituals can help provide mindfulness in your days. Before you get out of bed in the morning, give thanks for something—maybe even just for waking up to a new day. Before you go to sleep, give thanks for something that happened during the day. Open your heart. From a chakra standpoint, gratitude resides at the heart center. Our day-to-day activities tend to close in the heart a little, because we round our shoulders forward from working at the computer, driving, and doing everything else in front of us. When we slump forward, we literally hide the heart, obscuring this center for gratitude. The Yoga practices in month 3 that focus on placing the heart in an open position will be very helpful for experiencing more gratitude on a daily basis.

Gratitude journal

A journal to write down the things you are grateful for can help you get into the regular practice of gratitude. You can do this in any way that makes sense for you. Some people might give this more structure, such as writing down ten things they are grateful for per day. You can do it however you want. The idea is to spend some time thinking about and capturing what you are grateful for. I don't have a typical list, but here are some things I am grateful for:

- My dog sleeping on her pillow at my feet while I write
- The pizza Seth made for dinner last night
- My Yoga students

- That the espresso machine was broken a few weeks ago at a coffee shop I was in, which allowed me to discover Texas Gold tea, which I am now obsessed with
- Flowers on my tomato plants, indicating that I may finally get a tomato crop
- A quick chat with my son on the phone
- Curbside pickup at the grocery store
- My meditation practice
- My new blue shoes
- A text from my daughter
- Living in Austin
- Dark chocolate
- My teachers
- Emojis

Anything goes!

How to move forward with mindful gratitude

✓ Bring gratitude into daily activities. Be mindfully grateful for
  - Eating
  - Talking
  - Working
  - Commuting

- Relating
- Leisure activities

✓ Start and end your day in gratitude.
✓ Start and use a gratitude journal.

MINDFUL PRACTICE

1. Open your heart to gratitude in your Yoga practice. Backbends are particularly suited for this, and they are energizing too!
2. Surprise someone with a thank-you card or a verbal thank you.
3. Be grateful for your challenges.
4. Your gratitude list can be part of your daily journal, a list you keep on your phone, or anything at all.

Mindful Self-Care for the Holidays

Stay whole and happy during the holidays

*Take care of yourself to make room
for more joy in times of celebration.*

IF YOU ARE MOVING THROUGH this book month by month, you are now in the twelfth and final month, which, if you began in January, means you are in December—just in time for the holidays! Maybe you began in another month. That's okay too, of course. Just come back to this chapter at the time of the holidays.

Ah, the holiday season. . . .

TV shows and movies make the holidays look absolutely wonderful—families getting together and expressing their love to each other; delicious food and festive gatherings; decorated houses and a heartfelt exchange of gifts; newsletters and holiday cards to stay in touch and catch up. Over the river and through the woods...

Or maybe not. The holidays can be lovely, and when you practice some mindfulness, they really can be a time of reconnection with others, and with something bigger than yourself. However, this is also a time of year when our conditioning, expectations, and judgments take over; and those make it hard to keep the mindful perspective we have worked on so much over the year.

Leading up to the holidays, being too busy and being overwhelmed become the norm. Often the perfect Instagram-ready holidays don't bring the peace, love, and joy they promised. Instead, they bring *the seasonal stressors.*

Work, time, and finances
There might be sales goals to meet or other big projects to wrap up before everyone goes on vacation. This leads to longer hours, creating more of a sense of a time crunch. Bonuses might be on the line, which

leads to financial stress as well. Your heart may be in the right place, but you still feel stretched thin by year-end donation drives to worthy organizations.

Cards and gifts

Add to that the number of gifts that must be bought for extended family members, not to mention those holiday cards with the perfect, politically correct holiday greeting. How much do you share in the newsletter? Who stays on the list? Who drops off? Then add the time and cost of printing, stamping, and mailing. Set financial parameters. Most of us have some financial limits and can't spend indiscriminately. Prioritize. Speak up if you are in a situation where a contribution or party or gift-giving scenario is not comfortable for you.

Decorating, cooking, planning

Decorating pressure rears its head. You have a vision for what the ideal holiday looks like. If it involves a lot of work, and it often does, that often adds more time pressure. A bit of competition sometimes gets added in. If you are the busiest when prepping for the holidays, then your holidays are certainly going to be the best ... but we know that is not true. Rest. Make this a priority. Set a bedtime. Even if you are cooking, decorating, or planning, have a stopping point and honor it. If you are not rested, everything else suffers, as I talked about in month 4.

Parties

Some people live for parties. Others dread them. They suck up time you could spend meeting deadlines. You might be invited to too many, or maybe you're wondering why you weren't invited to any this year. What to wear, what to talk about, how much to eat and drink...

So much food

Lots of our favorite foods are ours for the taking around this time of year. We overeat and lament our tight clothing, bloating, and lack of energy. We over drink and feel dehydrated, headache-y, and tired the next day. Eat well. Be sure to nourish yourself during this time. Maintaining your mindful eating habits will help you be more in control at parties and gatherings. If you know you will be eating some of your favorite foods, embrace that and enjoy them, in moderation. As Mary Poppins told the young Banks children, "Enough is as good as a feast." Have enough.

Family gatherings

The Waltons? Not so much. Family relationships can be tricky. We revert to old roles and patterns. We look for the behaviors we expect to see and then get irritated when we find them. We have too much time with family or not enough. If we have to travel, we can run into bad weather, flight delays, and kids fighting in the backseat. Release unrealistic expectations. You may really wish you could have a reasonable discussion about politics with your uncle, but that may not happen. Or you may want everyone to love your new gluten-free cookies, but some people are going to make fun of them. And that's okay.

Look after yourself

I just painted a terrible picture of the holidays! I really love them, but I just want to point out that:

— Expectations run high.

— We are extra busy.

— We don't take care of ourselves.

And that can take its toll. Schedule self-care. Use your calendar and make appointments to take care of yourself. You may not be able to take a full spa day, but you can schedule an hour for Yoga, or a walk, or a nap, or whatever you need to feel taken care of during this time. Don't expect other people to do it for you.

Own your joy

It's helpful to move mindfully into the holiday season with perspective instead of expectation, and to take good care of yourself rather than sacrifice your health to create the perfect everything. This year, as the holiday season approaches, take a deep breath (or do any of the breathing exercises in month 2) and bring your mindful perspective into play. You have lots of tools, and you can do this.

We know we can't control anything outside ourselves. We can't control the weather, other people's attitudes and beliefs, or whether or not we will find the perfect gift. Plans change. All. The. Time. Based on your life, your passions, your relationships, and anything else, look at what can realistically happen. Prioritize. Let go of the rest.

Now that you have had quiet time to better understand yourself and regain perspective, you know a lot more about yourself than you did a year ago. Don't ignore what you have learned. You can "do you" at the holidays and everything will be okay. If you are doing something that doesn't mean anything to you, why are you doing it? Maybe it's because of a tradition and others love it. Maybe it's time to modify your involvement in that, or maybe it's time to create a new tradition that everyone will love. Trust your inner guidance and allow your true self to shine this holiday season.

How to move forward for mindful holidays

- ✓ Release unreasonable expectations.
- ✓ Let go of control.
- ✓ Don't overcommit.
- ✓ Set financial parameters.
- ✓ Eat well. If food is an issue during the holidays, make a plan so that you can really enjoy what you love without feeling guilty.
- ✓ Move. Even if you can't keep up with your regular exercise schedule during the holidays (or maybe you can if you plan for it), keep moving. Include walks in family gatherings. Get on the dance floor at parties. Resist staying on the couch for too long.
- ✓ Rest.
- ✓ Schedule self-care.

✓ Practice gratitude. During this time of year, gratitude can take your holiday joy to a whole new level!

✓ Be yourself.

✓ Connect and enjoy!

Ultimately, you want to move into the New Year with just as much hope, gratitude, and mindfulness as you had before the holidays. Great self-care can help you with this.

MINDFUL PRACTICE

Put more joy in your holiday season

1. Think about what triggers your holiday stress.
   — What are the triggers?
   — Why do these things trigger you?
   — What can you do to be ready for them?
   — How can you change your perspective?
2. What are your expectations of the holidays, and how does that lead to stress during this time of the year?
3. What things have you poured time and effort into in years past that you could let go of this holiday season? What might that make room for?

Mindfully Moving Forward

You can take it with you

It may be hard for an egg to turn into a bird; it would be a jolly sight harder for it to learn to fly while remaining an egg. We are like eggs at present. And you cannot go on indefinitely just being an egg. We must be hatched or go bad. — C. S. Lewis

AS WITH MOST THINGS, the more you practice them, the easier they get. Over time, it will take less and less effort to transition from a reactive state to a mindful outlook. Mindfulness is often buried under the expectations, beliefs, conditioning, and patterns you carry with you. Sometimes it is blurred by the chaos all around you, but it's there, and it will become more and more available within you. And now you know how to get back to it when it goes momentarily missing, or even when you feel you are having a mindfulness meltdown!

It is not always easy to bring a mindful perspective to every situation, but it is my hope that you now have some tools you are ready to use to move forward, along with a new perspective that will help you stress less, breathe more, be present, and feel better.

> *Peace is not the absence of anything. Real peace is the presence of something beautiful. Both peace and the thirst for it have been in the heart of every human being in every century and every civilization. — Maharaji*

Sometimes slower is better. As you move forward, you may want to only choose one or two areas to focus on at any time. Then, when that practice is fully integrated and you don't even have to think about it anymore, move on to work on something else. You will find that the process is not necessarily linear; it can circle around and back on itself.

Thanks to your new perspective, you can be really nice to yourself on this journey, and you can take comfort in the knowledge that there is no such thing as being good at mindfulness or achieving mindful perfection. The journey will not end, but you will feel more at home with yourself no matter where you are. This is a lifelong practice. These are tools to pack and there will be more to add on your way.

I wish you all the best on this grand adventure. Experience every moment. That is enough.

You are enough.

Lisa

Notes

1

[1] American Psychological Association 2017 Annual Survey http://www.apa.org/news/press/releases/stress/2017/state-nation.pdf

Month 5

[1] Source: http://www.dailyinfographic.com/15-terrifying-statistics-about-cell-phone-addiction

[2] https://www.psychologytoday.com/us/blog/mental-wealth/201402/gray-matters-too-much-screen-time-damages-the-brain

Month 7

[1] 2011 survey by human resources consulting firm Right Management

Month 7

[1] The iRest method is a guided meditation developed by Dr Richard Miller: www.irest.us

Acknowledgments

When I started my career in marketing and advertising some thirty years ago, I would have never imagined that my path would lead me to write this book. Everyone I have had the pleasure to know, and work with, and hang out with, and live with, has been a teacher to me along the way.

I am so grateful to my family, who has always supported me in whatever I endeavored to do. To Seth, who, without hesitation, encouraged me to take the leap from the more lucrative business world into the more experiential, holistic world of Yoga and mindfulness. To my children, Frank and Zoë, who watched me make the transition without even knowing what they were watching, came to my classes on Mother's Day, and always knew how important this was to me and cheered me on. To my mom and dad, who never second-guessed my decisions and allowed me to make them myself, showing me that they trusted my judgement. To my sisters, who, even though we don't see each other often, are always there when I need them. Thank you.

I've had so many wonderful teachers. My students, who may not know how much they have taught me, have been my motivation and inspiration, whether they came to one class or have been in my class for ten years. My teachers, who have helped me to stretch in new directions, even though at times I felt my head would explode with the flood of information and new concepts I have learned since beginning my Yoga studies. My wonderful friends, some of whom have known me since middle school and some who came into my adult life, who make my life really fun, listen to me, share with me, and laugh and laugh and laugh. Thank you.

Many, many people encouraged me to write this book. Many read drafts and gave ideas that improved the content greatly. Special thanks to Zoë and Seth, my first readers, as well as Jeana, Kevin, Allison, Melinda, Kelle, Lk, Leslie, Jennifer, Debbie, Theresa, Frank, Terry, Liz, Joshua, Tamar, and Sylvia for reading and for providing comments that were incredibly helpful. Thanks to Lynn and Jo, for sharing their experiences with this process.

Thanks to Anne Bannister for taking the photos and making the session fun. And to Freyja Zazu for turning me into art!

Thanks to my editor, Sally Hanan, for keeping things moving, and for being fiercely efficient with your revisions and comments. Your unwavering enthusiasm kept me going.

I hope you enjoyed this book and found it helpful in some ways. I hope that you will bring these ideas into your daily life and feel more present, calm, and at ease. And I hope that you will stay in touch and let me know what has contributed to any shifts that you make, should you choose to make them.

Be well,
Lisa

About the Author

Lisa Feder is a Yoga teacher, wellness consultant, and the founder of Being Well Yoga. After a twenty-five-year career in marketing and strategic planning, Lisa decided it was time to bring health and wellness to more people through Yoga. With Being Well Yoga, her mission is to bring Yoga and mindfulness education everywhere, including the workplace, making it easy for employees to rebalance during the workday and be calmer, more at ease, and even more productive.

Lisa has taught over 2,500 Yoga classes in all types of environments—from studios, to schools, to offices, to outdoor centers. She continues to teach studio classes and international retreats—so far to include

Costa Rica, Guatemala, Spain, and Italy. Bring your suggestions for the next one! She trains new Yoga teachers, speaks at conferences, and frequently gives workshops on stress management and mindfulness.

Lisa lives in Austin with her husband, Seth, and dog, Lucy, and spends her free time reading, hiking, dancing, cooking, and traveling. Her two adult children are now ruling the world from other cities, as they ought.

If you would like to contact Lisa for info about classes, speaking, retreats, book clubs, etc.:
WEBSITE: www.beingwellyoga.com
E-MAIL: lisa@beingwellyoga.com

Some Favorite Recipes

To get you started

White Bean Chili

    1 tablespoon olive oil

    2 cups diced yellow onion (about 2 medium)

    1 ½ tablespoons chili powder

    1 tablespoon minced garlic

    1 ½ teaspoons ground cumin

    1 teaspoon dried oregano

    3 (15.8-ounce) cans Great Northern beans, rinsed and drained (certified gluten-free if necessary)

    4 cups fat-free, less-sodium chicken broth

    3 cups chopped cooked turkey

    ½ cup diced, seeded plum tomato (about 1)

    1/3 cup chopped fresh cilantro

    2 tablespoons fresh lime juice

    ½ teaspoon salt

    ½ teaspoon freshly ground black pepper

    8 lime wedges (optional)

Heat oil in a large Dutch oven over medium-high heat. Add onion; sauté 10 minutes or until tender and golden. Add chili powder, garlic, and cumin; sauté for 2 minutes. Add oregano and beans; cook for 30 seconds. Add broth; bring to a simmer. Cook 20 minutes.

Place 2 cups of bean mixture in a blender or food processor and process until smooth. Return pureed mixture to pan. Add turkey and cook 5 minutes or until thoroughly heated. Remove from heat. Add diced tomato, chopped cilantro, lime juice, salt, and pepper, stirring well. Garnish with lime wedges, if desired.

Calories per cup: 281

Yellow Curry with Eggplant, Pepper, and Sweet Potato

3 cups coconut milk

1 cup vegetable stock

1 large sweet potato, peeled and cut into 1-inch pieces

1 red bell pepper, seeded and cut into 1-inch pieces

1 large Japanese eggplant, stemmed and cut into 1-inch pieces

1 tablespoon yellow curry paste

salt and ground pepper

Thai basil and cilantro for garnish

In a medium pot over medium-high heat, bring coconut milk and stock to a boil. Add the sweet potato and cook until tender 7–10 minutes. Add pepper, eggplant, and curry paste. Season with salt and pepper to taste. Simmer until vegetables soften, approximately 7 minutes. Serve over brown rice or rice noodles and garnish with cilantro and Thai basil.

Approximate calories per cup: 200

Quick and Easy Vegetable Soup

broccoli or zucchini or yellow squash,
butternut squash, kale, cauliflower (1 ½ cup
chopped)
¼ cup chopped leeks or onions
2 tbsp raw walnuts, cashews, almonds, or
pumpkin seeds

Steam the vegetables in a stainless-steel steamer for
3–5 minutes. Pour the vegetables, the steaming water,
and the nuts into a high-speed blender. Blend until
smooth. Season with Bragg Liquid Aminos, sea salt,
white pepper.

Approximate calories: 50–150, depending on how
many nuts you use

Spinach Lentil Soup

1 onion, chopped

2–3 stalks of celery, chopped

¾ cup of carrots, chopped

4–6 cloves of garlic, minced

¼ cup of olive oil

1 tsp each of dried oregano, basil, and cumin

½–1 tbsp red pepper flakes

2–3 bay leaves

1 15 oz can of crushed tomatoes

1 lb. bag of uncooked lentils

1 sweet potato, cubed

1 bag fresh spinach

salt, pepper

1 tbsp balsamic vinegar

8–10 cups of veggie broth, more if needed

Heat ¼ cup oil to medium heat. Add aromatics— onion, celery, carrots—and cook/stir until onions are tender. Add garlic, bay leaf, and other spices. Cook 2– 3 minutes, stirring often. Stir in vegetable broth, lentils, tomatoes, potatoes and bring to a boil. Reduce to a simmer & simmer 1 hr. Add salt & pepper to taste. Before serving, add/wilt spinach. Add 1 tbsp balsamic vinegar.

Approximate calories per cup: 150–200

Spinach Chana Masala

> 3 large onions, coarsely chopped
>
> 4–5 garlic cloves, minced
>
> 1–2 tbsp olive oil
>
> 1 tsp curry powder
>
> 1–2 tsp cumin
>
> 2 cups raw spinach
>
> 2 cans chickpeas, drained
>
> 2 cans peeled tomatoes, drained
>
> 1 can Amy's vegetarian chili
>
> chopped cilantro for garnish

Sauté the onions and garlic with the oil, curry powder, and cumin in a large pot until the onions are soft and translucent, approximately 5 minutes. Add the spinach until wilted. Add the chickpeas, tomatoes, and chili. Simmer for 20–30 minutes. Taste and add more spices if needed. Serve over rice and garnish with cilantro.

Approximate calories per cup: 275

Black Bean and Sweet Potato Enchiladas

12 oz can black beans (organic)

2 baked sweet potatoes (very soft)

1 tsp ghee

1 cup chopped leeks or onions

1 tsp black pepper

½ tsp red chili flakes

1 tbsp Bragg Liquid Aminos or tamari sauce

1 cup chopped spinach or chard

½ tsp cinnamon

1 tsp oregano

1 tsp cumin

Vegetable stock (as needed)

Nutritional yeast (optional)

Sky Valley Organic enchilada sauce, or homemade

12 corn tortillas

Rinse and drain the beans. Scoop the sweet potatoes out and discard the skins. Heat the ghee and add the leeks, pepper, chili flakes, and Bragg Liquid Aminos. Simmer for 2–3 minutes. Reduce heat and add the cooked black beans and sweet potatoes. Continue to simmer on low and add vegetable stock if the mixture becomes too dry (I usually add ¼ to ½ cup). Add the greens to the mixture as it continues to simmer. Add the remaining spices. Gently mash the ingredients together. Heat the tortillas in a sauté pan one at a time, adding a little vegetable broth to soften if desired. Pour some sauce into a 9 x 13-inch pan. Spread sauce on each tortilla and fill with the bean and potato mixture and nutritional yeast, if using, and roll up. Place in the pan seam side down. Pour the remaining sauce over the rolled tortillas and bake at 350° for 20–30 minutes. Top with freshly chopped cilantro. Makes 8–12 tortillas, depending on how full you make them. Can be made in a 9 x 13" pan (or experiment with other sizes, depending on how many batches you make!).

Approximately 175 calories per enchilada

Gluten-Free Veggie Lo Mein

7 oz. thin gluten-free spaghetti (even HEB has its own brand!)

1 cup vegetable broth

2 tbsp tamari, 2 tsp honey

½ tsp red pepper flakes, 1 tbsp grape seed oil

approximately 2 cups chopped veggies (broccoli, red pepper, scallions, mushrooms, or any others)

4 cloves minced garlic (or more if you like)

1 tbsp minced fresh ginger, pinch of kosher salt

1 tbsp roasted hemp seeds or sesame seeds

Cook pasta according to package directions (omitting any oil). Drain and set aside. In a bowl, combine the broth, tamari, and honey, whisking to dissolve. Add red pepper flakes. Heat a nonstick wok or large sauté pan over high heat. When the pan is hot, add the oil, heating until almost smoking. Add the vegetables and cook 2 minutes. Add garlic and ginger and sauté, stirring, for 2 minutes. Toss in the pasta, sprinkle with salt, and cook and stir until heated. Add the broth mixture and simmer, stirring often, for 4 minutes until the sauce has thickened. Transfer to serving platter and sprinkle with seeds.

Approximate calories per cup: 250

Kale with Raisins and Cashews

4 cups chopped kale, well washed

3 tbsp raisins

2 tbsp fresh lemon juice

2 tablespoons olive oil

¼ tsp salt

freshly ground black pepper

3 tbsp roughly chopped raw cashews

In a medium bowl, mix the kale with the lemon juice, olive oil, and salt. Gently massage the mixture into the kale. Mix in the raisins and season with black pepper. Let the mixture sit or refrigerate until serving. Toss the cashews in just before serving.

Calories per serving: 152 (serves 4)

Roasted Butternut Squash, Brussels Sprouts, and Onions*

1–2 cups cubed butternut squash

1–2 cups brussels sprouts

2 onions cut into quarters or large chunks

1 tbsp chopped fresh rosemary

½ tsp salt, freshly ground black pepper

½ tsp each ground nutmeg, cumin, cinnamon

Heat oven to 375°F. Place squash, onions, brussels sprouts, and rosemary on a rimmed baking tray coated with melted ghee. Cook until the squash and brussels sprouts are slightly browned and begin to caramelize. This could take 30 minutes or a little more or less. Stir tray with a spatula every 5–10 minutes to ensure even cooking. Remove from the oven and toss with the rest of the spices.

*I use all kinds of vegetables with this—feel free to experiment—broccoli, cauliflower, mushrooms, any kind of squash, sweet potatoes. The length of time needed to cook the vegetables will vary—I usually let them cook a long time. Even if some vegetables get very soft, they still taste great.

Approximate calories per cup: 150

Coconut-Almond-Oatmeal Banana Cookies

2 cups unsalted roasted almonds

1 cup melted coconut oil

¾ cup maple syrup

2 large eggs (or flaxseed replacement)

1 tsp vanilla extract

1 small ripe banana, mashed

2 ½ cups rolled oats, gluten free

½ cup dried cherries, raisins, or chopped apricots

Preheat oven to 350°F. Place almonds in a food processor and grind finely; set aside. Using a blender, blend the coconut oil, maple syrup, eggs, and vanilla. In a large mixing bowl, beat the banana, oats, and ground almonds with a mixer. Add the coconut oil mixture and stir until well combined. Add the dried fruit, if using, and mix it in. Drop rounded tablespoons on a nonstick cooking sheet lined with parchment paper. Bake for 12 minutes or until lightly browned. Transfer to a cooling rack.

Gluten-Free Fudgy Brownies

1 ½ cups black beans, drained

½ cup cooked and mashed sweet potato

2 tbsp coconut oil

10 large medjool dates, pitted and chopped

½ cup applesauce

1 ½ tsp vanilla extract

¼ or more cup honey

¾ cup gluten-free flour mix

½ cup organic cocoa

1 tsp baking powder

¼ tsp salt

½ cup chopped walnuts

Preheat oven to 350°F. Lightly oil an 8 x 8" glass cooking pan. In the bowl of a food processor, combine beans, sweet potatoes, coconut oil, dates, applesauce, vanilla, and honey. Puree until very smooth. In a large bowl, sift together flour, cocoa, baking powder, and salt. Stir in wet ingredients to blend well. Batter will be very thick. Taste batter and add 2 tbsp honey if it is not sweet enough. Stir in walnuts. Transfer batter to prepared baking dish and bake until batter is set, about 40 minutes. Let cool, then cut into squares and serve.